READY SET ★ STAAR

FOR TEXAS
SCIENCE SUCCESS

NATIONAL
GEOGRAPHIC

School Publishing

PROGRAM CONSULTANTS

Randy Bell, Ph.D.

Kathy Cabe Trundle, Ph.D.

Judith S. Lederman, Ph.D.

David W. Moore, Ph.D.

Grade **5**

REPORTING CATEGORY 1
MATTER AND ENERGY

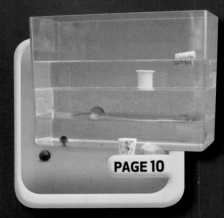

PAGE 18

PAGE 22

PAGE 24

Grade 5

REPORTING CATEGORY 2

FORCE, *MOTION,* AND ENERGY

PAGE 28

PAGE 34

POPCORN

PAGE 38

PAGE 42

PAGE 68

PAGE 72

PAGE 78

PAGE 80

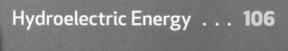

PAGE 110

PAGE 114

PAGE 116

PAGE 120

PAGE 126

Grade **5**

REPORTING CATEGORY 4

ORGANISMS AND ENVIRONMENTS

PAGE 148

PAGE 154

PAGE 160

PAGE 158

PAGE 176

PAGE 192

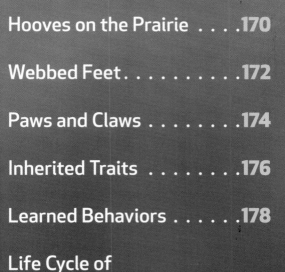
PAGE 188

400,000 volts of electricity travel long distances from power plants. But electric appliances in your home run on 220 or 110 volts. A transformer, such as this one, reduces the voltage. Smaller transformers on poles or in utility boxes reduce the voltage even more before the electricity reaches your home.

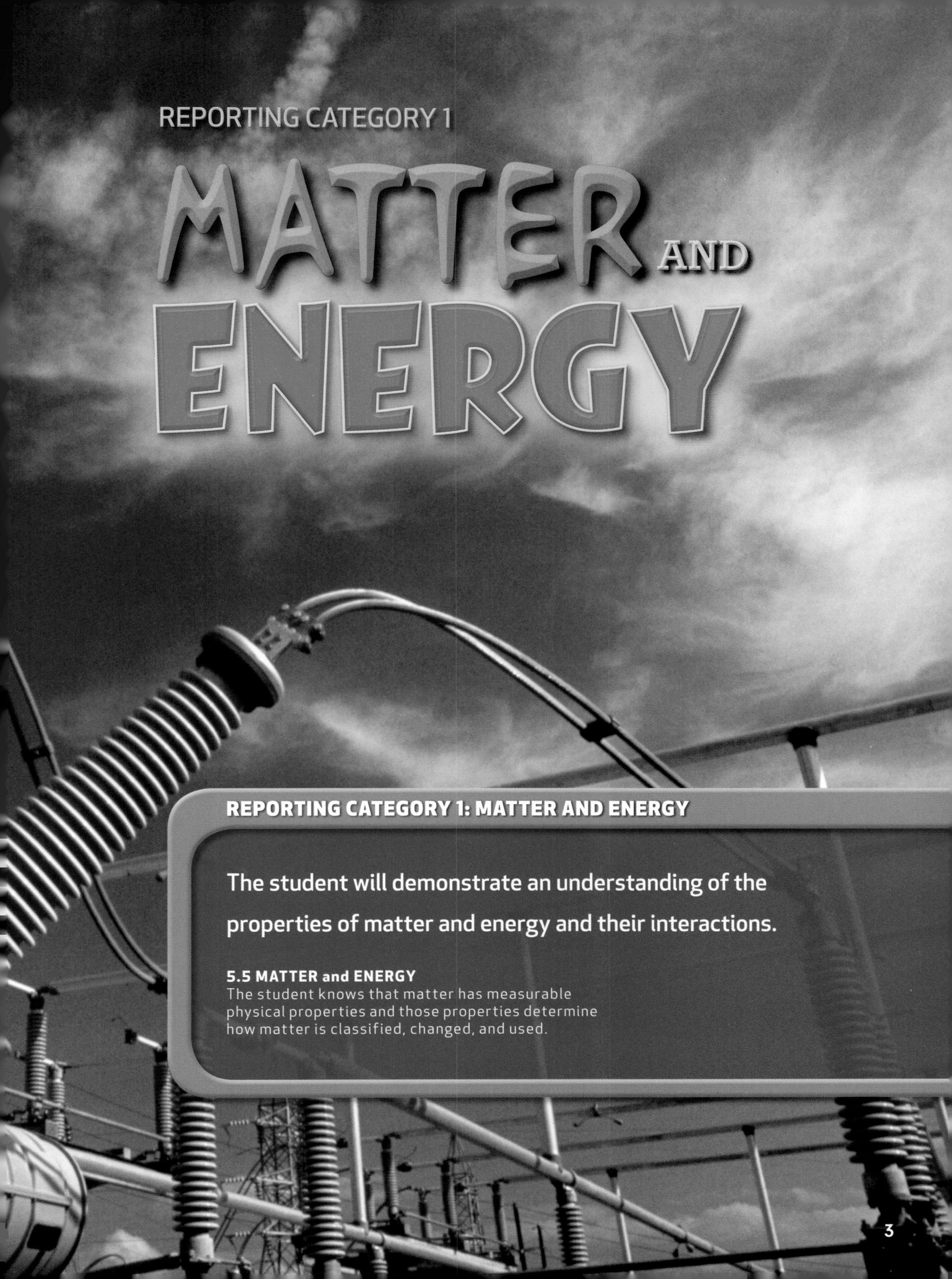

MATTER AND ENERGY

REPORTING CATEGORY 1: MATTER AND ENERGY

The student will demonstrate an understanding of the properties of matter and energy and their interactions.

5.5 MATTER and ENERGY

The student knows that matter has measurable physical properties and those properties determine how matter is classified, changed, and used.

MASS

How do scientists define **matter?** Matter is anything that has **mass** and takes up space. Mass is the amount of matter in an object. Scientists describe and compare matter based on properties, or qualities. Objects can be classified based on properties of matter, such as mass.

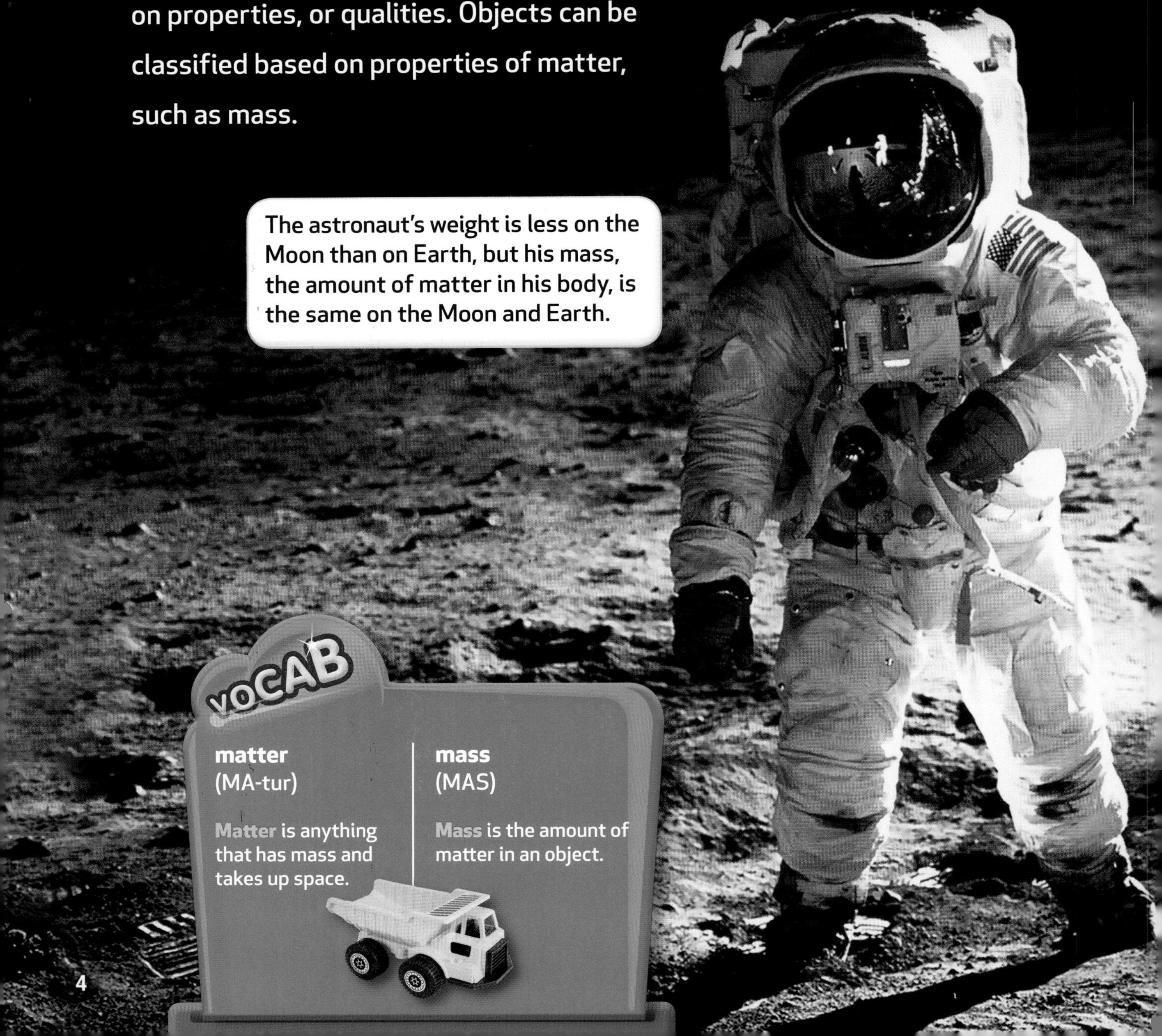

The astronaut's weight is less on the Moon than on Earth, but his mass, the amount of matter in his body, is the same on the Moon and Earth.

voCAB

matter
(MA-tur)

Matter is anything that has mass and takes up space.

mass
(MAS)

Mass is the amount of matter in an object.

READY SET STAAR

READINESS STANDARD TEKS 5.5.A:
Classify matter based on physical properties, including mass, magnetism, physical state (solid, liquid, and gas), relative density (sinking and floating), solubility in water, and the ability to conduct or insulate thermal energy or electric energy.

Some large objects, such as the truck shown in the photo, have a large mass. Smaller objects, such as the toy truck, may have a much smaller mass. Sometimes objects that are similar in size can have very different masses. For example, a brick has more mass than a sponge of the same size. A steel ball has more mass than a foam ball of the same size.

toy truck

dump truck

This toy dump truck is made up of very little matter. It has a small mass.

This dump truck is made up of a lot of matter. It has a large mass.

my science notebook

WRAP IT UP!

1. **Define** What is mass?

2. **Classify** Choose four objects in your classroom. Classify the objects based on their mass.

3. **Classify** Sort the following animals into groups according to mass: elephant, mouse, camel, chipmunk, raccoon, hippopotamus.

MAGNETISM

Another way that matter can be classified is based on a force called **magnetism**. Magnetism is a force produced by magnets that pulls some metals. Objects can be classified based on whether or not they are attracted to a magnet.

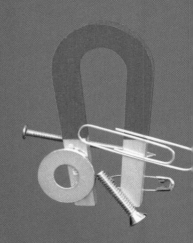

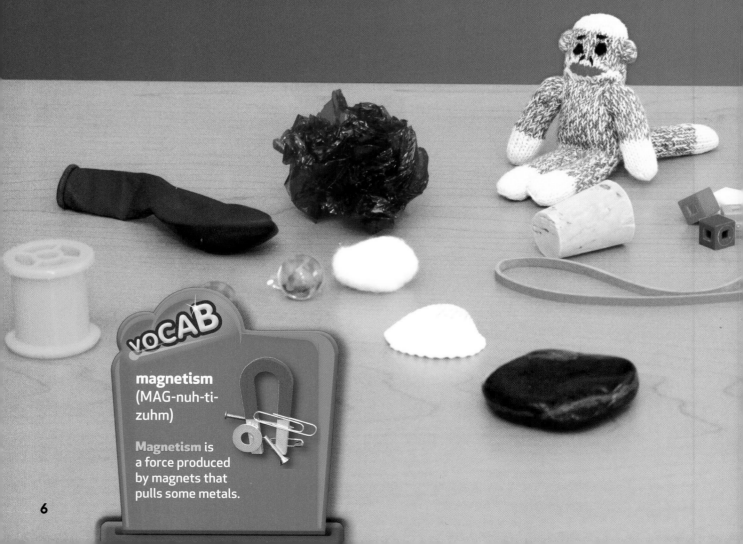

voCAB

magnetism
(MAG-nuh-ti-zuhm)

Magnetism is a force produced by magnets that pulls some metals.

READINESS STANDARD TEKS 5.5.A: Classify matter based on physical properties, including mass, magnetism, physical state (solid, liquid, and gas), relative density (sinking and floating), solubility in water, and the ability to conduct or insulate thermal energy or electric energy.

Look at the photograph of the objects on the table. Notice that some of the objects are attracted to the magnet. Observe that other objects remain on the table. Some metal objects, such as paper clips and iron nails, are magnetic. Other metal objects, such as pennies, are non-magnetic. What other objects in the photo can be classified as non-magnetic?

All of these objects can be classified as magnetic or non-magnetic. The magnetic objects are attracted to the magnet, while the non-magnetic objects are not.

My science *notebook* **WRAP IT UP!**

1. **Define** What is magnetism?

2. **Classify** Sort the following objects into groups based on their magnetic properties: penny, metal paper clip, cork, iron nail, marble.

7

SOLIDS, LIQUIDS, and GASES

Solids, liquids, and gases are physical states of matter. Matter can be classified by its physical state. For example, a brick has a definite shape. A brick is a solid.

Liquids, such as milk in a carton or bottle, take the shape of their containers. Liquids do not necessarily fill a container completely.

If you have ever seen a balloon floating in the air, you have seen an object filled with gas. Gases have no definite shape. Gases spread out to completely fill a space.

READINESS STANDARD TEKS 5.5.A:
Classify matter based on physical properties, including mass, magnetism, physical state (solid, liquid, and gas), relative density (sinking and floating), solubility in water, and the ability to conduct or insulate thermal energy or electric energy.

The surfboard is a solid. The ocean is a liquid. Air is a gas. Moving air, or wind, can push objects, such as this sail.

My science notebook

WRAP IT UP!

1. **Compare and Contrast** How are liquids and gases alike? How are they different?

2. **Classify** Find examples of solids, liquids, and gases in your classroom. Explain how you classified each of the objects as a solid, liquid, or a gas.

WHAT FLOATS? WHAT SINKS?

Scientists can classify matter based on its relative density. **Density** is the measure of the amount of matter in a certain amount of space. An object's density determines whether it will sink or float. Look at the photo. The liquid with the least density is at the top of the container. The liquid with the greatest density is at the bottom. The vegetable oil floats on top of water because its density is less than the density of water.

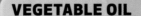

VEGETABLE OIL

WATER

CORN SYRUP

voCAB

density
(DEN-si-tē)

Density is the measure of the amount of matter in a certain amount of space.

READY SET STAAR

READINESS STANDARD TEKS 5.5.A: Classify matter based on physical properties, including mass, magnetism, physical state (solid, liquid, and gas), relative density (sinking and floating), solubility in water, and the ability to conduct or insulate thermal energy or electric energy.

Objects can be classified by their density, too. The density of the plastic spool is greater than the density of vegetable oil but less than the density of water. The cork has the least density of all the matter in the photo. It floats in the vegetable oil. The marble has the greatest density. It sinks to the bottom of the corn syrup.

By comparing which objects float and which objects sink, matter can be classified based on its relative density.

My science notebook

WRAP IT UP!

1. **Describe** Look at the cherry in the container. Describe the cherry's density in relation to water and corn syrup.

2. **Classify** A peeled orange sinks in water, but an unpeeled orange floats. What can you conclude about their relative densities?

INVESTIGATE
SOLUBILITY
in
WATER

 Which materials dissolve in water?

If you stir a spoonful of sugar into a glass of water, the sugar dissolves. The mixture of sugar and water is a solution. You can no longer see the particles of sugar. The dissolved particles are distributed evenly throughout the solution. In this investigation, you can observe whether some other materials are soluble, or can dissolve, in water.

MATERIALS

4 plastic cups with water   sand   plastic spoon

salt   25 mL lemon juice   25 mL vegetable oil

READY SET STAAR

SUPPORTING STANDARD TEKS 5.5.D:
Identify changes that can occur in the physical properties of the ingredients of solutions such as dissolving salt in water or adding lemon juice to water. (Also 5.5.A)

1

Predict what will happen when sand is added to water. Add a half spoonful of sand to a cup with water. Stir the water with a spoon for about 30 seconds. Record your observations in your science notebook.

My science notebook

2

Predict what will happen when salt is added to water. Add a half spoonful of salt to a cup with water. Stir the salt and water for about 30 seconds. Record your observations.

3

Predict what will happen when lemon juice is added to water. Pour 25 mL lemon juice into a cup with water. Stir the lemon juice and water for about 30 seconds. Record your observations.

4

Predict what will happen when vegetable oil is added to water. Pour 25 mL vegetable oil into a cup with water. Stir the vegetable oil and water for about 30 seconds. Record your observations.

My science notebook

WRAP IT UP !

1. **Predict** Did your results support your predictions? Explain.

2. **Describe** How did the physical properties of the salt and the lemon juice change when they were added to water?

3. **Classify** Sort the materials you used in this investigation into groups based on their solubility in water.

13

THERMAL CONDUCTORS AND INSULATORS

Matter is made up of particles that are always vibrating, or moving. The energy of moving particles is **thermal energy.** The ability of matter to conduct thermal energy is a property of matter. Matter can be classified based on how well it conducts thermal energy. Good conductors of thermal energy, or **thermal conductors,** allow thermal energy to flow through them easily. Metals such as copper, aluminum, and iron are good thermal conductors.

VOCAB

thermal energy
(THUR-mul EN-ur-jē)

Thermal energy is the energy of vibrating, or moving, particles.

thermal conductor
(THUR-mul
kon-DUK-ter)

A **thermal conductor** is a material that heats up quickly.

thermal insulator
(THUR-mul
IN-su-lā-ter)

A **thermal insulator** is a material that heats up slowly.

READINESS STANDARD TEKS 5.5.A: Classify matter based on physical properties, including mass, magnetism, physical state (solid, liquid, and gas), relative density (sinking and floating), solubility in water, and the ability to conduct or insulate thermal energy or electric energy.

Cloth, wood, and rubber objects do not conduct thermal energy well. These materials are **thermal insulators.** We can use these materials to protect us from hot objects, such as a pot on a stove. Glass, plastic, and leather are other materials that are good thermal insulators.

THERMAL CONDUCTORS

The metal rod on the thermometer conducts thermal energy.

Iron is a good thermal conductor. Many pots and pans are made of metals, including iron.

THERMAL INSULATORS

This spatula is made of wood. Wood is a good thermal insulator.

Potholders are made of cloth. Cloth is a good thermal insulator.

Materials such as plastic and fireproof fabric are good thermal insulators. They are used to make safety clothing for these firefighters.

My science notebook **WRAP IT UP !**

1. **Contrast** What is the difference between a thermal conductor and a thermal insulator?

2. **Classify** Identify the following materials as thermal conductors or thermal insulators: a wooden spoon, an iron frying pan, a plastic spatula, a steel fork.

15

ELECTRICAL CONDUCTORS
AND INSULATORS

Have you ever seen a spark when you touched a doorknob on a dry day? If so, you have seen charged particles moving. The energy of moving charged particles is **electrical energy.** Electrical energy can move through wires. Think about a lamp. Electrical energy moves along wires to the lamp and lights the bulb. The ability of matter to conduct electrical energy is a property of matter. Matter can be classified based on how well it conducts electrical energy. Good conductors of electrical energy, or **electrical conductors,** allow electricity to flow easily. Metals such as copper, gold, silver, and iron are good electrical conductors.

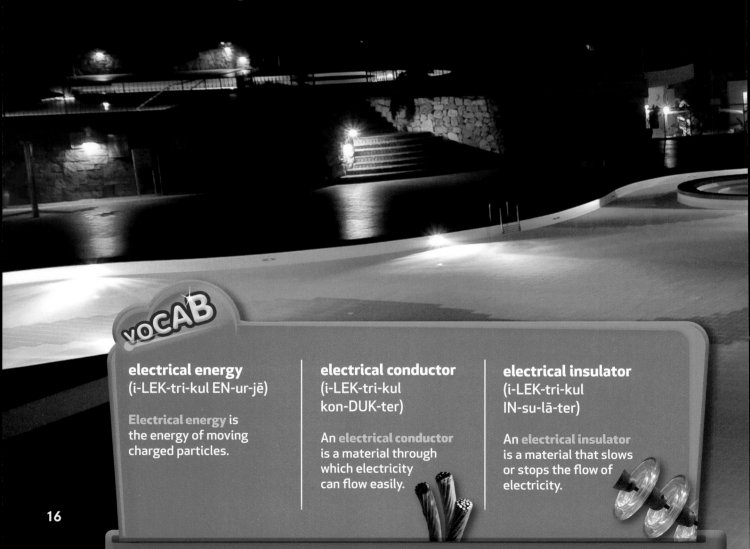

vocAB

electrical energy
(i-LEK-tri-kul EN-ur-jē)

Electrical energy is the energy of moving charged particles.

electrical conductor
(i-LEK-tri-kul kon-DUK-ter)

An electrical conductor is a material through which electricity can flow easily.

electrical insulator
(i-LEK-tri-kul IN-su-lā-ter)

An electrical insulator is a material that slows or stops the flow of electricity.

READINESS STANDARD TEKS 5.5.A:
Classify matter based on physical properties, including mass, magnetism, physical state (solid, liquid, and gas), relative density (sinking and floating), solubility in water, and the ability to conduct or insulate thermal energy or electric energy.

Because electricity can be dangerous, it is important to protect people from it. An **electrical insulator** can do this. An electrical insulator is a material that slows or stops the flow of electricity. Plastic, rubber, wood, and glass are good electrical insulators.

ELECTRICAL CONDUCTORS

Copper wires carry electricity in power lines and electrical plugs.

Gold carries electricity in some parts of a computer.

ELECTRICAL INSULATORS

Plastic coating on wires helps to prevent electical shocks.

Glass electrical insulators prevent electricity from reaching a person working on power poles.

Electrical insulators cover the lights and pumps in this pool. The lights and pumps are powered by electricity.

My science notebook

WRAP IT UP!

1. **Define**   What is electrical energy?

2. **Contrast**   What is the difference between an electrical conductor and an electrical insulator?

3. **Classify**   Which is a better electrical conductor, copper or plastic? Explain.

BOILING, FREEZING, and MELTING

One of the most important substances on Earth is water. Water can be found on Earth as a solid, a liquid, and a gas. Look at the photo of water boiling in a pot. Bubbles are forming. The water is changing from a liquid to a gas called water vapor. When a liquid boils, it changes to a gas. At a temperature of 100 degrees on the Celsius scale, water boils and becomes water vapor. The temperature 100°C is the boiling point of water.

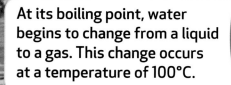

At its boiling point, water begins to change from a liquid to a gas. This change occurs at a temperature of 100°C.

Yellowstone National Park has many geysers. In the right conditions, the water underground reaches its boiling point and the geyser erupts.

SUPPORTING STANDARD TEKS 5.5.B:
Identify the boiling and freezing/melting
points of water on the Celsius scale.

The change from liquid to soild is called freezing. If the temperature of liquid water decreases to 0° Celsius, water begins to freeze. The melting point of water is also 0°C. If the temperature of ice rises to 0°C, ice begins to melt.

The freezing point of water is 0 degrees on the Celsius scale. The melting point of water is also 0°C.

My science notebook — WRAP IT UP!

1. **Identify** What temperature is the freezing and melting point of water?

2. **Describe** What happens to water when it reaches a temperature of 100°C? What is this temperature called?

19

INVESTIGATE
PROPERTIES OF
WATER

? How do cooling and heating affect properties of water?

Water can be a solid, a liquid, or a gas, depending on its temperature. Water changes between these three states of matter when cooled and heated. In this investigation, you will observe how the cooling and heating of water can cause its physical properties to change.

MATERIALS

2 plastic bags

tape

graduated cylinder

water

READY SET STAAR

SUPPORTING STANDARD TEKS 3.5.C:
Predict, observe, and record changes in the
state of matter caused by heating or cooling.

1 Label 2 plastic bags Bag 1 and Bag 2. Use a graduated cylinder to measure 100 mL of water. Pour the water into a bag. Seal the bag. Repeat with the other bag.

Bag 1

2 *My science notebook*

Place the bags in a freezer. Predict what will happen to the water. Record your prediction in your science notebook. The next day, take the bags out of the freezer. Turn the bags in different directions. Record your observations.

3 Put the bags on your desk. Wait 30 minutes. Turn the bags in different directions. Record your observations.

4 Put the bags in sunlight. Open Bag 1. Predict what will happen to the water in the bags after 3 days. Observe the bags every day for 3 days. Record your observations.

My science notebook

WRAP IT UP!

1. **Predict** Did your results support your predictions? Explain.

2. **Explain** In what ways did the properties of the water change when it was cooled and heated?

INVESTIGATE MIXTURES

 What happens to properties of iron and sand when they are mixed together?

In a mixture, there are two or more kinds of matter put together. Materials can maintain their physical properties when they are combined in a mixture. In this investigation, you will observe the physical properties of iron filings and sand when they are combined in a mixture.

MATERIALS

plastic bag with sand

plastic bag with iron filings

plastic bag with mixture of iron filings and sand

hand lens

magnet

READY SET STAAR

SUPPORTING STANDARD TEKS 5.5.C: Demonstrate that some mixtures maintain physical properties of their ingredients such as iron filings and sand.

1

Observe the contents of each bag with a hand lens. Record your observations in your science notebook.

2

Move the magnet across the bag of sand. Record your observations. Move the magnet across the bag of iron filings. Record your observations.

3

Predict what will happen when you move the magnet across a bag of iron filings and sand. Record your predictions.

4

Move the magnet across the bag of iron filings and sand. Record your observations.

My science notebook

WRAP IT UP!

1. **Predict** Did your results support your predictions? Explain.

2. **Explain** What physical properties of the iron filings and sand did not change when they were combined in a mixture?

23

PHYSICAL CHEMIST

Rod Ruoff

Rod Ruoff is a physical chemist. He works at the University of Texas at Austin. He also started a company where he works with his team to research new ways of making energy. The team uses materials with interesting properties.

NG Science: What do you currently study?

Rod Ruoff: My team and I study properties of materials. We can then classify the materials based on their properties. We think about how these materials can make society better.

NG Science: What type of research have you done?

Rod Ruoff: At first, I studied tiny pieces of matter to learn about how they stick together. Now I mostly research materials made of carbon. Diamonds are made of carbon, and so is graphite. Graphite is the same material as the "lead" in your pencil. Individual layers of graphite are called "graphene" and we study atom-thick layers of this material. I want to make materials that can help our environment.

This is what graphene looks like when magnified. Graphene is a special type of graphite. Graphene is 200 times as strong as steel.

graphene

Graphene can be used in solar power cells. Graphene is so thin, it lets light through.

Force! Motion! Energy! All are evident at the Texas State Fair in Dallas, Texas, home of the Texas Star Ferris wheel. At a height of 64.6 meters (212 feet), the Ferris wheel weighs over 308,000 kilograms (nearly 680,000 pounds). It can make 1.5 revolutions per minute and can carry up to 264 passengers.

REPORTING CATEGORY 2

FORCE, MOTION, AND ENERGY

REPORTING CATEGORY 2: FORCE, MOTION, AND ENERGY

The student will demonstrate an understanding of force, motion, and energy and their relationships.

5.6 FORCE, MOTION, and ENERGY
The student knows that energy occurs in many forms and can be observed in cycles, patterns, and systems.

SPIN IT!

Texas produces more electricity from wind than any other state. The **mechanical energy** in wind can be used to produce electrical energy. Look at the photograph of the wind turbines. The energy of the wind causes the blades of the wind turbines to turn around and around. The moving blades of the turbines have mechanical energy because of their motion. People can use the mechanical energy of the turbines to produce electricity.

voCAB

mechanical energy
(mi-KAN-i-kul EN-ur-jē)

Mechanical energy includes energy an object has because of its motion.

Wind turbines on a wind farm change mechanical energy into electricity.

READINESS STANDARD TEKS 5.6.A:
Explore the uses of energy, including mechanical, light, thermal, electrical, and sound energy.

The energy from the moving blades of the wind turbines runs a generator. The generator changes the mechanical energy of the wind and moving blades into electricity. People can use this electricity in homes, schools, and offices.

Water turbines change the mechanical energy from moving water in the ocean into electricity people can use.

 **WRAP IT UP!**

1. **Define** What is mechanical energy?

2. **Explain** How is the mechanical energy from the moving blades of the turbines used to produce electricity?

29

LIGHT IT UP!

What objects can you think of that give off light? **Light energy** travels through empty space and includes energy that you can see. Look at the photograph of the light show. People use a special kind of light, a laser light, in the show. What makes laser light so special? It is not like regular light from a bulb. It is not like the natural light from the Sun. Laser light does not have different colors of light. Each laser is only one color. To produce a laser light show, many different colored lasers are used.

These people are watching a laser light show. Each laser only produces one color of light.

VOCAB

light energy
(LĪT EN-ur-jē)

Light energy travels through empty space and includes energy that you can see.

READY SET STAAR

READINESS STANDARD TEKS 5.6.A: Explore the uses of energy, including mechanical, light, thermal, electrical, and sound energy.

Light energy that you can see can be used in many other ways, too. People use light from sources such as lamps, streetlights, and flashlights to see objects. Light from computers and television screens can help you get information or enjoy your favorite show.

A laser can be used to read bar codes on items in a factory or supermarket.

Plants need light energy to grow. These plants are grown indoors using a special kind of light.

People use light energy to illuminate buildings. The city of Austin, Texas, is a spectacular display of light energy.

My science notebook

WRAP IT UP!

1. **Define** What is light energy?

2. **Recall** What are two uses of light energy from lasers?

3. **Evaluate** Make a list of ways you use light energy in one day. What use of light do you think is most important? Explain.

HOW LIGHT TRAVELS

? How can you use a flashlight to demonstrate how light travels?

Think about using a flashlight to find an object in a dark room. How do you move the flashlight to find the object? How can you find the object if it is behind another object? In this investigation, you will use a flashlight to observe how light travels.

MATERIALS

2 index cards with holes | 1 index card without a hole | 3 pieces of clay | flashlight

READY SET STAAR

READINESS STANDARD TEKS 5.6.C: Demonstrate that light travels in a straight line until it strikes an object or travels through one medium to another and demonstrate that light can be reflected such as the use of mirrors or other shiny surfaces and refracted such as the appearance of an object when observed through water.

1 Place each index card into a piece of clay. Put a card with a hole in front of a card without a hole.

2 Shine a flashlight through the hole in the first card. Observe the second card. Record your observations in your science notebook.

My science notebook

3 Place the other card with a hole in front of the first card. Move the card until you can shine the light through the two holes. Record your observations.

4 Move the second card slightly to one side. Shine the flashlight through the hole in the first card. Record your observations.

My science notebook

WRAP IT UP !

1. **Explain** How did the cards need to be arranged for light to pass through the holes in both cards?

2. **Conclude** Does light travel in a straight line, or can it bend around objects? Explain.

33

REFLECT ON IT!

Light travels in a straight line. When you see an object, light is **reflecting,** or bouncing, off of that object. You can only see an object when light reflects off the object and back to your eyes. Some objects with smooth, shiny surfaces, such as mirrors or glass, reflect an image that you can see. Look at the picture below. Because the outside of the building is made of smooth, shiny glass, you can see a reflection of the buildings across the street and of the sky.

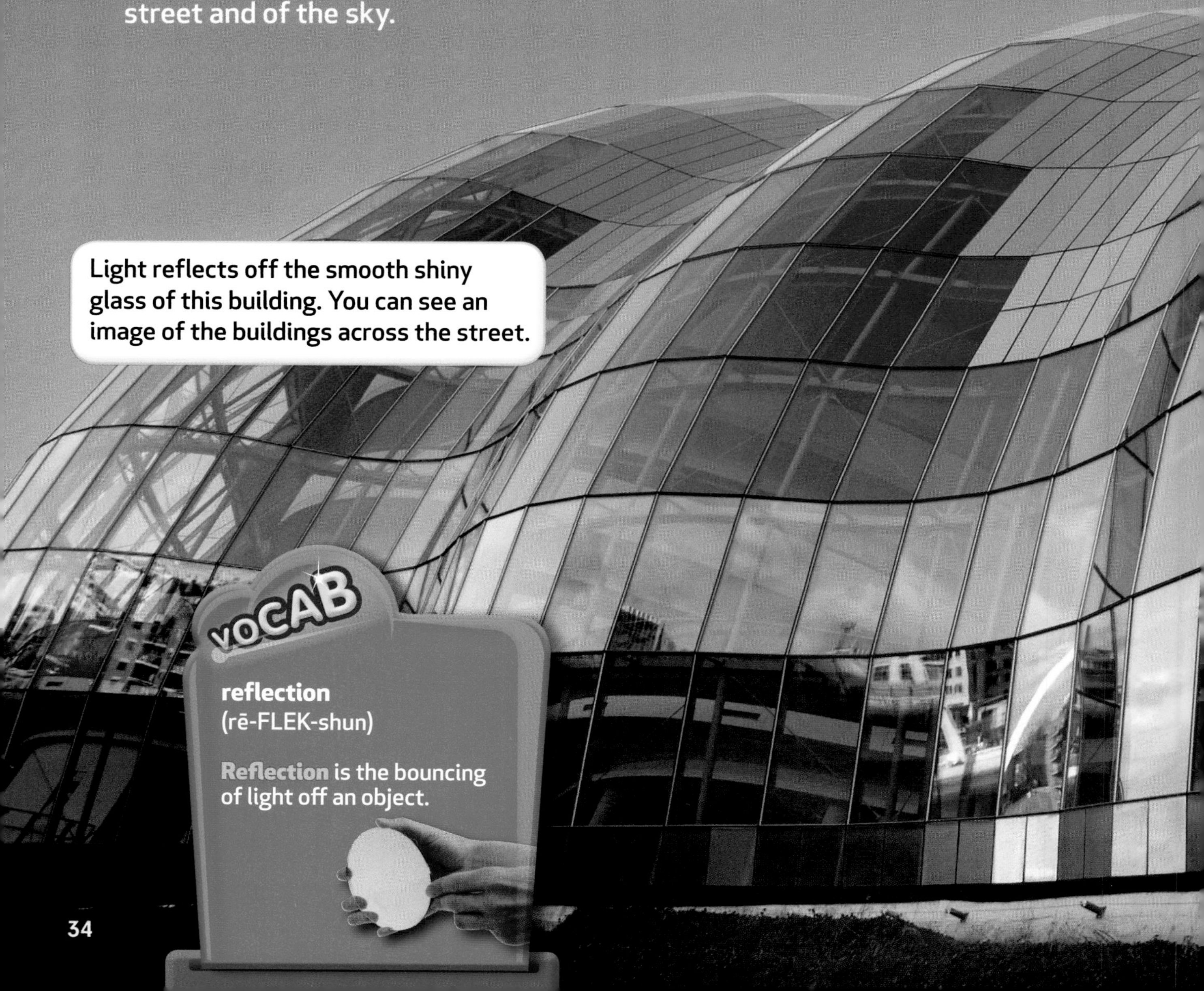

Light reflects off the smooth shiny glass of this building. You can see an image of the buildings across the street.

voCAB

reflection
(rē-FLEK-shun)

Reflection is the bouncing of light off an object.

READINESS STANDARD TEKS 5.6.C:
Demonstrate that light travels in a straight line until it strikes an object or travels through one medium to another and demonstrate that light can be reflected such as the use of mirrors or other shiny surfaces and refracted such as the appearance of an object when observed through water.

Science in a Snap!

Reflection

Draw a circle on an index card. Place an index card on your desk and hold a mirror above the card.

Shine a flashlight onto the shiny side of the mirror. Try to get the light from the flashlight to reflect into the circle on the card.

? **What did you have to do to get the light to shine in the circle? What happened to the light when it struck the mirror?**

My science notebook

WRAP IT UP!

1. **Define** What is reflection?

2. **Recall** What happens to light when it strikes a mirror?

3. **Apply** On what other shiny surfaces can you see a reflection of yourself?

35

REFRACTION

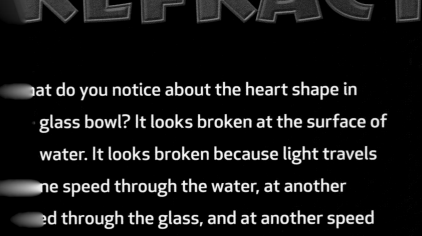

hat do you notice about the heart shape in glass bowl? It looks broken at the surface of water. It looks broken because light travels ne speed through the water, at another ed through the glass, and at another speed ugh the air. Light bends, or **refracts,** it passes from the water through the to the air.

This heart shape looks like it is in two parts because the light is refracted. The light changes direction as it travels from water, through the glass, to air.

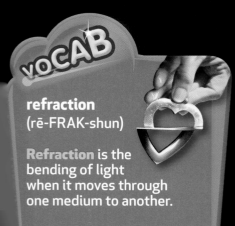

voCAB

refraction
(rē-FRAK-shun)

Refraction is the bending of light when it moves through one medium to another.

READINESS STANDARD TEKS 5.6.C:
Demonstrate that light travels in a straight
line until it strikes an object or travels through
one medium to another and demonstrate that
light can be reflected such as the use of mirrors
or other shiny surfaces and refracted such as
the appearance of an object when observed
through water.

Science in a Snap!

Refraction Action

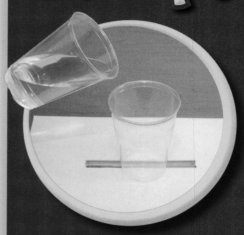

Use markers and a ruler to draw parallel lines of different colors on a piece of paper. Place a clear cup on the lines. Observe how the lines appear through the empty cup.

Add water until the cup is half full. Observe again.

 How do the lines appear to change? Explain what happened to the light as it traveled from the lines to your eyes.

My science notebook WRAP IT UP!

1. **Define** What is refraction?

2. **Compare** How is refraction different from reflection?

3. **Apply** Your friend places a straw in a glass of water. It looks like the straw is in two parts. Why does the straw look this way?

37

HEAT IT UP!

The particles that make up matter are always vibrating or moving. The energy of the moving particles is **thermal energy.** People use thermal energy in many ways. One way that people use thermal energy is by making a campfire. This camper is sitting by a campfire on a cool, dark night. The campfire helps keep the camper warm. The camper can keep his drink warm using thermal energy from the campfire, too.

This camper uses thermal energy from the campfire to stay warm in this cold climate.

voCAB

thermal energy
(THUR-mul EN-ur-jē)

Thermal energy is the energy of vibrating, or moving, particles.

READINESS STANDARD TEKS 5.6.A:
Explore the uses of energy, including mechanical, light, thermal, electrical, and sound energy.

Thermal energy can be used in many other ways. Thermal energy is used to heat buildings. You probably dry your clothes using thermal energy from a clothes dryer. Look at the photos of objects that use thermal energy. Do you use either of these objects?

Warm air from a hair dryer causes water from wet hair to evaporate.

This popcorn maker heats popcorn seeds until they pop out of the hard outer shells.

My science notebook

WRAP IT UP!

1. **Define** What is thermal energy?

2. **Recall** How can people use thermal energy from a campfire?

3. **Apply** You have learned about some uses of thermal energy. What other ways do you use thermal energy every day?

SOUND THE ALARM!

Sound energy is produced by vibrations and includes energy that you can hear. One way that people use sound energy is to alert others in a weather emergency. Look at the photo of the tornado. Tornadoes can be very destructive. Warning sirens, like the one in the photo, can help warn people that tornadoes have been spotted near their homes. The warning siren alerts people to go to a safe place, such as a basement or shelter.

This warning siren signals that tornadoes have been seen in an area.

Gruver, Texas, has a warning siren that alerted its citizens when this tornado touched down north of the city.

voCAB

sound energy
(SOWND EN-ur-jē)

Sound energy is produced by vibrations and includes energy that you can hear.

READINESS STANDARD TEKS 5.6.A:
Explore the uses of energy, including
mechanical, light, thermal, electrical,
and sound energy.

People use sound energy in many ways in their everyday lives, too. Police and other emergency personnel use sirens to alert people to make way for emergency vehicles. You may wake up with an alarm from your clock each morning. A doorbell is used to alert people that someone is at their door. Even telephones use sound to let you know that someone is calling.

Many people use alarm clocks to alert them that it is time to wake up for school or work.

Police use a loud siren as a warning that they are on their way to an emergency.

My science notebook

WRAP IT UP !

1. **Define** What is sound energy?

2. **Recall** How do warning sirens help keep people safe?

3. **Apply** You have learned about some uses of sound energy. What other ways do you use sound energy every day?

IT'S ELECTRIC!

You probably know that to get the light bulb in a lamp to light, you need to plug the cord into an electrical outlet and turn on the switch. To produce light, the lamp uses **electrical energy.** Electrical energy is the energy of moving charged particles. Electrical energy can travel as electric current through wires to complete a circuit. Look at the photograph of the many lights along the Riverwalk in San Antonio, Texas. What makes all this happen? Electricity!

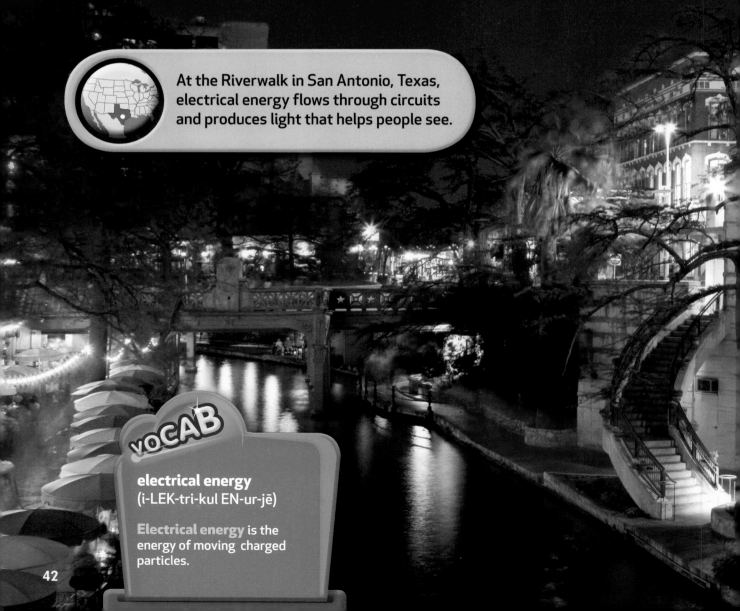

At the Riverwalk in San Antonio, Texas, electrical energy flows through circuits and produces light that helps people see.

vOCAB

electrical energy
(i-LEK-tri-kul EN-ur-jē)

Electrical energy is the energy of moving charged particles.

READINESS STANDARD TEKS 5.6.A:
Explore the uses of energy, including mechanical, light, thermal, electrical, and sound energy.

READINESS STANDARD TEKS 5.6.B:
Demonstrate that the flow of electricity in circuits requires a complete path through which an electric current can pass and can produce light, heat, and sound.

One way that people use electrical energy is to produce other useful forms of energy such as light, heat, and sound. If you see light in a room, feel heat from a space heater, or hear sound from a radio, you know how useful electrical energy is.

Electric current flows through a circuit and produces heat in a waffle iron.

The electric guitar is attached to an amplifier. The amplifier makes the sound from the guitar louder.

My science notebook

WRAP IT UP!

1. **Define** What is electrical energy?

2. **Recall** Give examples of how electrical current passing through a circuit can be used to produce light, heat, and sound.

3. **Apply** You have learned about some uses of electrical energy. What other ways do you use electrical energy every day?

43

ELECTRICAL CIRCUITS

The colorful lights in the picture run on electricity. The wires and lights make up an **electrical circuit.** An electrical circuit is a complete path through which electric current can pass. A battery or an outlet into which you can plug a cord are sources of electricity for circuits.

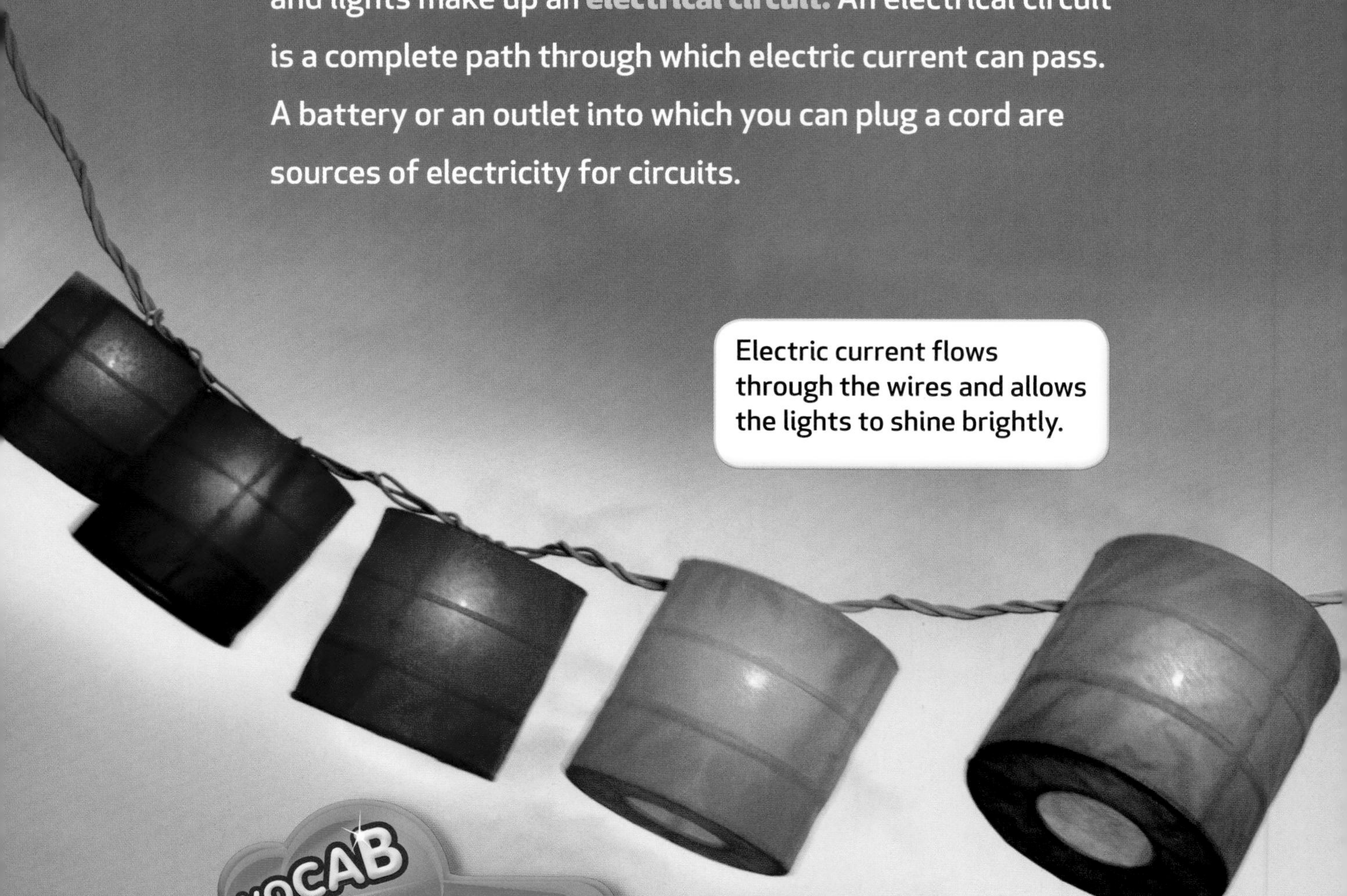

Electric current flows through the wires and allows the lights to shine brightly.

voCAB

electrical circuit
(i-LEK-tri-kul SUR-kuht)

An **electrical circuit** is a complete path through which electric current can pass.

READINESS STANDARD TEKS 5.6.B:
Demonstrate the flow of electricity in circuits requires a complete path through which an electric current can pass and can produce light, heat, and sound.

A battery has stored energy. The battery has a positive end and a negative end. If you attach a wire from one end of the battery to the other, you create a complete path through which an electric current can pass. For the current to flow, the circuit must be complete. If the wire is not connected to both ends of the battery, the electricity cannot pass through the circuit.

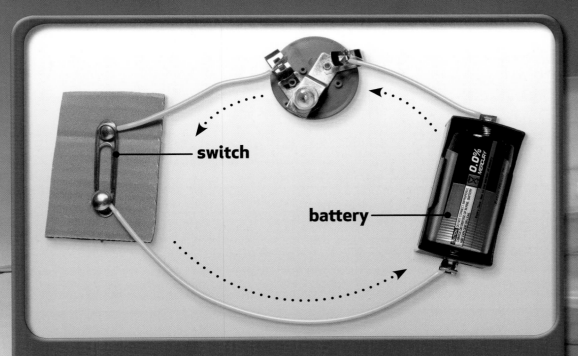

switch

battery

Trace the path through which electricity flows in the circuit. When the wires are connected and the switch is closed, there is a complete path through which an electric current can pass. Then the light bulb lights up.

WRAP IT UP !

1. **Define** What is an electrical circuit?

2. **Infer** What happens to the flow of electric current when you flip a light switch to off? Explain.

INVESTIGATE

CIRCUITS

 Which materials can complete an electrical circuit?

For electricity to flow, a circuit must be complete. The electric current can flow and light a bulb. In this investigation, you can find out which materials can complete an electrical circuit.

MATERIALS

light bulb in holder

battery in holder

3 wires

materials to test

1

Attach wires to a battery holder and to a bulb holder as shown.

2

My science notebook

Notice that there are two wire ends that are not connected. Touch the ends of the wires together to make a complete circuit. Record your observations in your science notebook.

3

Predict whether a rubber band will complete the circuit if you touch the wire ends to it. Record your prediction. Touch the ends of the wires to the rubber band. Record your observations.

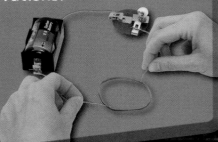

4

Predict whether other materials will complete the circuit. Record your predictions. Test the materials. Record your observations.

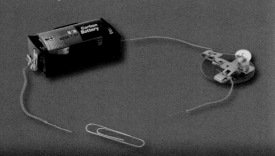

My science notebook

WRAP IT UP!

1. **Predict** Did your results support your predictions? Explain.

2. **Describe** What materials are needed to build a complete circuit? How are the materials used to complete the circuit?

47

PEDAL POWER!

Do you enjoy riding your bike? What you might not know is that scientists consider riding a bicycle to be work. In science, work is done when force is used to move an object over a distance. Each time you push down on the pedals of your bicycle, the bicycle moves, or changes position. Since the bicycle moves because of the force that you applied, riding a bicycle is doing work.

Bicyclists use the pulley in their bicycles to get to the top of the mountain. Riding a bicycle may be fun, but it is still work!

voCAB

work
(WERK)

Work is done when a force is used to move an object over a distance.

pulley
(PUL-lē)

A pulley is a grooved wheel with a cable or a rope running through the groove.

SUPPORTING STANDARD TEKS 3.6.B:
Demonstrate and observe how position and
motion can be changed by pushing and pulling
objects to show work being done such as
swings, balls, pulleys, and wagons.

Bicycles use a special pulley. A pulley is a grooved wheel with a cable or rope running through the groove. In the case of a bicycle, the pulley consists of a bicycle chain and a gear wheel. Pulleys often lift objects upward, but in this case, the pulley moves the rider forward whenever he or she applies force to the pedals. The force causes the bicycle to move, or change position, so the rider is doing work.

This gear wheel works as a pulley. The chain takes the place of a rope that would be part of a regular pulley.

My science notebook

WRAP IT UP!

1. **Define** What is work?

2. **Explain** How is using the pulley to make a bicycle move an example of work being done?

3. **Apply** Think of any activity that you do at home. It might be closing a door or opening a book. Explain whether that activity is work, and why.

INVESTIGATE
PULLEYS

? How can you use a pulley to move an object?

You can pull on the rope of a pulley to move an object and do work.
Pulleys are often used to change direction of motion or move an
object that is some distance away from you. In this investigation,
you can use a pulley to show how to move a flag.

MATERIALS

2 large rubber bands

tape

marker

foam board with spools

SUPPORTING STANDARD TEKS 3.6.B:
Demonstrate and observe how position and
motion can be changed by pushing and pulling
objects to show work being done such as
swings, balls, pulleys, and wagons.

1 Wrap tape around a rubber band to make a flag. Use a marker to make a pattern on the flag. Place the rubber band on spools attached to a foam board.

2 Turn the spools and pull the rubber band in different directions. Observe how the flag moves. Record your observations in your science notebook.

My science notebook

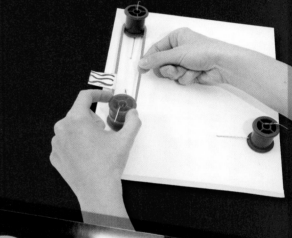

3 Place another rubber band on two spools. Predict how the flag will move when you move the spools and pull the rubber band in different directions. Record your prediction.

4 Turn the spools and pull the rubber band in different directions. Record your observations.

My science notebook

WRAP IT UP!

1. **Predict** Did your results support your predictions? Explain.

2. **Explain** Describe how the flag moved when you turned the spools and pulled the rubber bands in different directions.

51

KEEP ON MOVING!

Work can be done when playing sports and games. In bowling, you do work when you push the ball to make it roll down a lane. Rolling the ball down the lane puts the ball in motion, which is a change in position. The ball then hits the pins and knocks them down. Work is done when the ball moves and knocks over the pins.

The bowling ball is doing work. It pushes the pins, knocking them down. Strike!

SUPPORTING STANDARD TEKS 3.6.B:
Demonstrate and observe how position and
motion can be changed by pushing and pulling
objects to show work being done such as
swings, balls, pulleys, and wagons.

Work can be done with other objects, too. The man with the luggage cart is doing work. He is pushing the luggage cart and making it move. Since he is using a force, a push, and the luggage cart is in motion, work is being done. How is the woman pushing the swing doing work?

This man is doing work. He applies force to the luggage cart to put it in motion. The luggage cart works like a wagon.

When the woman uses a force to put the swing in motion, work is being done.

My science notebook

WRAP IT UP!

1. **Explain** How is bowling an example of work being done?

2. **Explain** How is using a luggage cart to move a suitcase an example of work being done?

3. **Generalize** If you try to push a shopping cart but cannot make it move, has work been done? Explain.

EXPERIMENT
FORCE ON AN OBJECT

One type of investigation that scientists do is an **experiment.**
An experiment is an investigation in which **variables** are manipulated
and controlled. A variable is something that can change in an experiment.
The following pages give instructions for doing an experiment.

Magnetic force is used in the experiment. When you hold two magnets
together with different poles next to each other, they attract each other.
When you hold two magnets together with the same poles next to each
other, they repel each other. You can do an experiment to test the effect
of different masses on the motion caused by the force of magnets.

voCAB

experiment
(ex-PAIR-i-ment)

An **experiment** is
an investigation in
which variables are
manipulated and
controlled.

variable
(VAIR-ē-u-bul)

A **variable** is
something that
can change in an
experiment.

Follow the instructions to do an experiment. Then use the experiment as a guide to design your own experiment that tests the effect of force on an object.

☑ ASK A QUESTION. GATHER MATERIALS.

FORCE ON AN OBJECT

My science notebook

QUESTION

How does adding mass to a toy car affect the distance the toy car is moved by the force of magnets?

This question can be answered using materials that are safe and easy to obtain.

MATERIALS

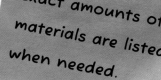

2 bar magnets
toy car
tape
ruler
10 pennies

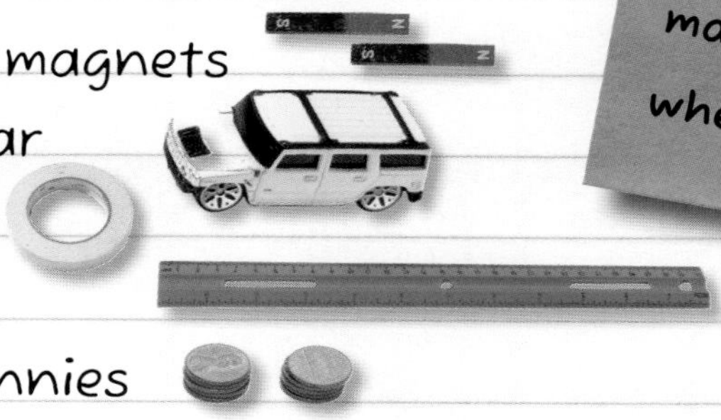

Exact amounts of materials are listed when needed.

☑ FORMULATE A HYPOTHESIS.

A **hypothesis** is a statement that gives a possible answer to a question that can be tested by an experiment. A hypothesis can be written using an "If . . . , then . . ." statement.

HYPOTHESIS

My science notebook

You can use an "If . . . , then . . ." statement to make your hypothesis clear.

If mass is added to a toy car, then the distance the toy car is moved by the force of magnets will decrease.

SUPPORTING STANDARD TEKS 5.6
Design an experiment that tests the ef
force on an object.

☑ IDENTIFY, MANIPULATE, AND CONTROL VARIABLES.

Choose one variable that you will change in the experiment.

Then describe which variable you will observe or measure.

Keep all other variables the same.

Answer these three questions:
1. What one thing will I change?
2. What will I observe or measure?
3. What things will I keep the same?

VARIABLE TO CHANGE

My science notebook

The number of pennies that are placed on the toy car will change in each trial. The mass will increase by adding more pennies.

VARIABLE TO OBSERVE OR MEASURE

The distance the toy car is moved by the force of magnets will be measured.

VARIABLES TO KEEP THE SAME

Use the same toy car in each trial. Use the same magnets and keep the surface the same. Hold the magnet and release the car the same way each time.

MAKE A PLAN. THEN CARRY OUT YOUR PLAN.

Plan the steps for the experiment. Write the steps in order.
Be sure the steps are written clearly.

PLAN

1. Tape a bar magnet to the top of the toy car with the north pole of the magnet pointing toward the back of the car.

2. Line up the back of the toy car with the 0 end of the ruler. Hold the car in place. Hold the north pole of the other magnet next to the north pole of the magnet attached to the car.

Write detailed plans. Another student should be able to repeat your investigation without asking any questions.

SUPPORTING STANDARD TEKS 5.6.D:
Design an experiment that tests the effect of
force on an object.

PLAN CONTINUED

My science notebook

3. Release the car. Measure the distance
the car moves. Record your data in your
science notebook.

4. To add mass, place 5 pennies
on top of the magnet on the
toy car. Then repeat steps 2
and 3.

5. To add more mass, place 5 more pennies
on top of magnet on the toy car. Then
repeat steps 2 and 3 one more time.

COLLECT AND RECORD DATA.

Record your data in a table like this one.

Effect of Mass on Distance Moved

	Number of Pennies Added	Distance the Toy Car Moved
Trial 1	0	
Trial 2	5	
Trial 3	10	

 # ANALYZE DATA.

Use the data you collected to make a graph. Look for patterns in the data. What happened to the distance the toy car moved each time pennies were added?

Describe what happened based on the data you collected.

SUPPORTING STANDARD TEKS 5.6.D:
Design an experiment that tests the effect of
force on an object.

✓ EXPLAIN AND SHARE RESULTS.

Explain the steps of the experiment and the results to the class.
Use the graph to show patterns in the data. Tell what happened to
the distance the car moved in each trial.

✓ TELL WHAT YOU CONCLUDE.

Answer the experiment question. Tell how adding mass to the toy car
affected the distance the toy car was moved by the force of magnets.

✓ DESIGN YOUR OWN EXPERIMENT.

Choose one of these questions, or make up your own question.
1. How does adding even more mass affect the distance a
   toy car is moved by the force of magnets?
2. How does changing the surface a toy car is on affect the
   distance the toy car is moved by the force of magnets?
3. How does changing the force from a push to a pull affect
   the distance a toy car is moved by the force of magnets?

WRAP IT UP!

1. **Define** What is a hypothesis?

2. **Explain** Why is it important to test only one variable
   at a time in an experiment?

3. **Explain** When you designed your own experiment, what
   variable did you change? What variable did you observe
   or measure? What variables did you keep the same?

61

ANIMAL SOUND EXPERT

Dr. William Conner

Dr. William Conner and his team at Wake Forest University have been studying how animals use sound energy. They collect the sounds with video cameras and very sensitive microphones.

NG Science: What do you do in your job?

Dr. Conner: I study signals animals produce, how they travel through the environment, and the messages they give. My students and I have been studying the battle of sounds between insects and bats that prey on them.

NG Science: What are you trying to learn about the sounds animals make?

Dr. Conner: We know that bats use sound when they track tiger moths to eat. Tiger moths can answer the signals that bats make by making high-pitched clicking noises. These noises confuse the bats, and make it hard for them to hunt the moths.

NG Science: What is your favorite part of your job?

Dr. Conner: Observing animal behaviors and hearing sounds for the first time makes my job something to look forward to every day.

★ READY SET STAAR

TEKS 5.3.D:
Connect grade-level appropriate science concepts with the history of science, science careers, and contributions of scientists.

Special nighttime cameras capture the animals' actions in the dark.

Bats use their hearing more than they use their sight to find insects to eat.

Balanced Rock, in the Guadalupe Mountains National Park in Texas, seems to defy gravity. In the distance, the mountain peak, El Capitan, rises out of the Chihuahuan Desert. El Capitan is part of an ancient limestone reef. This area was once part of a huge sea.

REPORTING CATEGORY 3

EARTH AND SPACE

REPORTING CATEGORY 3: EARTH AND SPACE

The student will demonstrate an understanding of components, cycles, patterns, and natural events of Earth and space systems.

5.7 EARTH and SPACE
The student knows that Earth's surface is constantly changing and consists of useful resources.

5.8 EARTH and SPACE
The student knows that there are recognizable patterns in the natural world and among the Sun, Earth, and Moon system.

LANDFORMS

Earth's surface is made up of different types of **landforms.** A landform is a natural feature. All over Earth you can see landforms, such as **deltas, canyons,** and **sand dunes.** You might think that these features never change, but they do. Slowly over time, water and ice carve canyons into the land and widen river deltas. Wind pushes sand dunes across the desert floor. Quick changes happen too. Landslides tear into hills and mountains. Volcanoes suddenly erupt. The chart on the next page shows some landforms that are the result of changes to Earth's surface.

SAND DUNES

Sand dunes, such as the ones in this picture, are hills of sand formed by wind.

The Sahara, North Africa

VOCAB

landform
(LAND-form)

A **landform** is a natural feature on Earth's surface.

delta
(DEL-tuh)

A **delta** is new land that forms at the mouth of a river.

canyon
(KAN-yen)

A **canyon** is a deep, narrow valley with steep sides that is formed by flowing water.

DELTAS

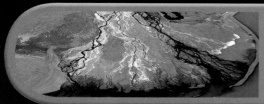

A delta is new land that forms at the mouth of a river.
Delta on Lake Tekapo, New Zealand

CANYONS

A canyon is a deep, narrow valley with steep sides that is formed by flowing water. *Grand Canyon, Arizona, USA*

MOUNTAINS

Mountains are high places with steep sides that rise above surrounding land. *The Himalaya, Bhutan*

PLAINS

A plain is a large flat area of land.
Plains in Kansas, USA

U-SHAPE VALLEYS

A U-shaped valley is formed by a glacier. *Dawes Glacier, Alaska, USA*

sand dune
(SAND DŪN)

A **sand dune** is a hill of sand formed by wind.

My science notebook

WRAP IT UP!

1. **Identify** Name one landform caused by wind and one landform caused by water.

2. **Explain** How are some landforms related to changes to Earth's surface?

67

WEATHERING

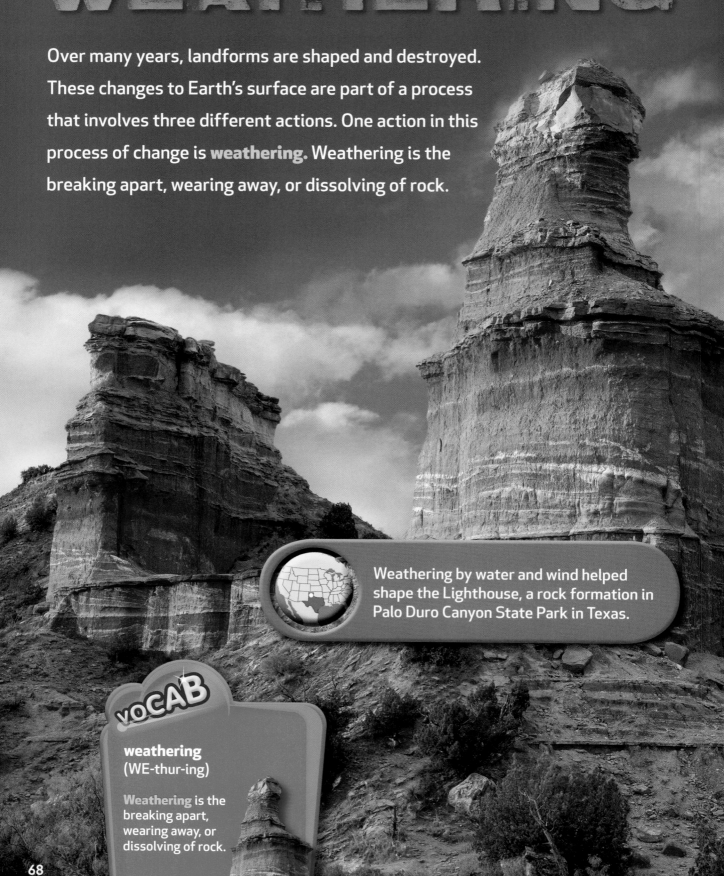

Over many years, landforms are shaped and destroyed. These changes to Earth's surface are part of a process that involves three different actions. One action in this process of change is **weathering**. Weathering is the breaking apart, wearing away, or dissolving of rock.

Weathering by water and wind helped shape the Lighthouse, a rock formation in Palo Duro Canyon State Park in Texas.

voCAB

weathering
(WE-thur-ing)

Weathering is the breaking apart, wearing away, or dissolving of rock.

READINESS STANDARD TEKS 5.7.B: Recognize how landforms such as deltas, canyons, and sand dunes are the result of changes to Earth's surface by wind, water, and ice.

People can observe weathering in the cracks in rocks and on the surface of rocks that have been rubbed smooth by wind or flowing water. Wind, water, ice, chemicals, and even plants can cause weathering. Landforms are the result of changes to Earth's surface. Many of these changes began with the weathering of rock.

HOW A CAVE FORMS

Water containing acid seeps into the cracks in limestone.

The acid dissolves the limestone, eventually forming a cave.

The Rio Camuy Cave in Puerto Rico formed from water that seeped into cracks in limestone. Acid in the water dissolved the limestone, eventually forming a cave.

My science notebook

WRAP IT UP!

1. **Recall** What can cause weathering?

2. **Explain** Describe how weathering might change rocks.

3. **Cause and Effect** How does water contribute to the formation of a cave?

69

EROSION AND DEPOSITION

Weathering produces a lot of sediment, or loose material such as boulders, pebbles, and sand. What happens to these pieces of rock? Often, they are moved to a new place. The moving of sediment from one place to another is called erosion. Wind, water, ice, and gravity all can move sediment from one place to another, causing erosion and changes to Earth's surface.

voCAB

sediment
(SED-ah-mint)

Sediment is material that comes from the weathering of rock.

erosion
(ē-RŌ-zhun)

Erosion is the picking up and moving of rocks and soil to a new place.

deposition
(de-pō-ZI-shun)

Deposition is the laying down of rock and soil in a new place.

READINESS STANDARD TEKS 5.7.B:
Recognize how landforms such as deltas, canyons, and sand dunes are the result of changes to Earth's surface by wind, water, and ice.

What happens to the sediment that is carried away? It is dropped in a new place in a process called deposition. The soil that erodes from a hill might be deposited, or dropped, at the bottom of the hill. Look at the photo of the different sizes of sediment on Deer Isle in Maine. The photo shows sediment that has been eroded and deposited. The processes of erosion and deposition cause changes to Earth's surface.

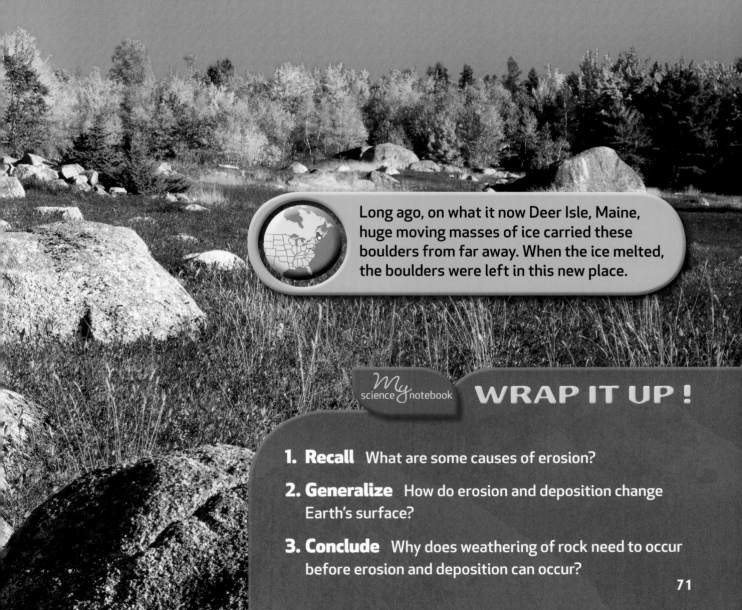

Long ago, on what it now Deer Isle, Maine, huge moving masses of ice carried these boulders from far away. When the ice melted, the boulders were left in this new place.

My science notebook WRAP IT UP!

1. **Recall** What are some causes of erosion?

2. **Generalize** How do erosion and deposition change Earth's surface?

3. **Conclude** Why does weathering of rock need to occur before erosion and deposition can occur?

71

BUILDING SAND DUNES

Wind can change Earth's surface through weathering, erosion, and deposition. Wind picks up and moves small pieces of sediment such as sand. Some of the sand may slam into rocks, making the rocks smooth. If conditions are right, grains of sand can collect and build into a sand dune. A sand dune is a landform that results from wind changing Earth's surface.

Sand can collect into a sand dune where grains of sand crash into an object that blocks their forward motion. The object may be a rock, a plant, a hill, or even a house.

READY SET STAAR

READINESS STANDARD TEKS 5.7.B: Recognize how landforms such as deltas, canyons, and sand dunes are the result of changes to Earth's surface by wind, water, and ice.

Sand dunes form in windy places where sand is plentiful, such as on a beach or in a desert. Steady winds push grains of sand along the ground, changing Earth's surface. Some of the grains of sand slam into objects, such as rocks or plants, that block their movement along the ground. A sand dune forms as more and more grains of sand slam into an object and become trapped. Over time, a sand dune may grow very tall.

SAND MOUNTAINS

How tall can a sand dune get? A few of Earth's tallest sand dunes reach heights of more than 500 meters (1640 feet).

Sand dunes in Guadalupe Mountains National Park, Texas

My science notebook **WRAP IT UP!**

1. **Recall** Where do sand dunes usually form?

2. **Cause and Effect** What causes sand dunes?

3. **Generalize** How are sand dunes a result of changes to Earth's surface by wind?

73

CARVING CANYONS

Moving water can change Earth's surface in a big way. For example, the Rio Grande formed the canyon pictured below. How does moving water change Earth's surface? Like wind, moving water carries sediment, such as sand and gravel. Sediment carried by the Rio Grande scraped and chipped away rock on the sides and bottom of the river. It took many years for the river to carve this canyon.

Over time, the Rio Grande eroded enough rock to form this canyon.

READINESS STANDARD TEKS 5.7.B:
Recognize how landforms such as deltas, canyons, and sand dunes are the result of changes to Earth's surface by wind, water, and ice.

If you hiked from the canyon rim to the river's edge, you might see that many of the rocks are smooth and rounded. Sediment, carried along by the water, bumps and rubs against larger rocks. Eventually, the surface of the rocks wears away. The rocks become smoother, more rounded, and smaller. Weathering and erosion may be slow processes, but over time, they can make huge changes to Earth's surface.

The rushing water in the Rio Grande weathers rocks, making them smoother.

WRAP IT UP !

My science notebook

1. **Identify** Which process forms canyons, erosion or deposition? Explain.

2. **Explain** How can weathering and erosion change the surface of rocks?

3. **Generalize** How are canyons a result of changes to Earth's surface by water?

DEPOSITING DELTAS

Water moves sediment from one place to another, changing Earth's surface. Rivers often move soil and rock as they flow toward lakes or the ocean. Where does all of that sediment end up? Some of it is deposited at the mouth of the river, the place where the river empties into the ocean. Given enough time, the sediment can build up to form a delta—new land that forms at the mouth of a river. Deltas are landforms that result from changes to Earth's surface by water.

The Mississippi River delta is at the mouth of the river where the river empties into the ocean.

READINESS STANDARD TEKS 5.7.B:
Recognize how landforms such as deltas, canyons, and sand dunes are the result of changes to Earth's surface by wind, water, and ice.

Deltas form because fast-moving water can carry more sediment than slow-moving water. As a stream or river slows down, it deposits some of the sediment it was carrying. For example, the Mississippi River slows down as it flows into the ocean. The slowed river water deposits sediment. The sediment has gradually built up to form the Mississippi River delta.

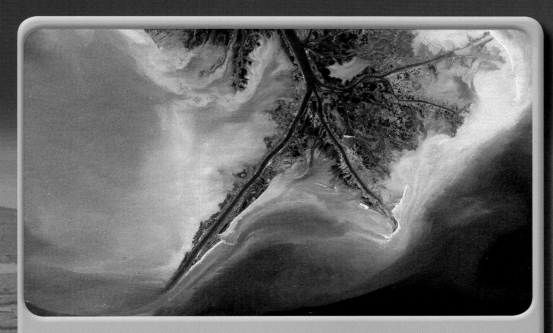

Long ago, this land that forms the Mississippi River delta did not exist. The delta formed over thousands of years as the river deposited more and more sediment.

WRAP IT UP!

1. **Recall** What is a delta?

2. **Generalize** How are deltas a result of changes to Earth's surface by water?

3. **Infer** How might a delta form where a river empties into a lake?

77

EARTH AND ICE

What can move rocks that are as big as a house and as small as a grain of sand? Ice! In some places, massive glaciers changed Earth's surface as they slowly moved over the land. A glacier is a huge area of slow-moving ice. As glaciers moved, they picked up rocks and carried them along. Over time, the glaciers melted and retreated. The sediment carried by the glaciers was left behind.

Many of the landforms in Yosemite Valley, such as the hanging valleys and steep cliffs, were carved out by glaciers.

READY SET STAAR ★

READINESS STANDARD TEKS 5.7.B:
Recognize how landforms such as deltas, canyons, and sand dunes are the result of changes to Earth's surface by wind, water, and ice.

Ice can change Earth's surface in another way, too. Water that seeps into cracks in a rock freezes and expands. The ice inside the cracks acts like a wedge, making the cracks wider. The repeated freezing and thawing of water breaks the rock apart.

hanging valley

glacial polish

U-shaped valley

A hanging valley is a valley formed by a small, shallow glacier that flowed into a larger glacier. Bridalveil Fall flows from a hanging valley in Yosemite.

Long ago, a glacier scraped this rock in Yosemite until it was smooth and polished.

As powerful glaciers moved into this area of Yosemite, the glaciers carved deep, wide U-shaped valleys.

My science notebook

WRAP IT UP!

1. **Compare** How are erosion and deposition by a river like erosion and deposition by a glacier?

2. **Explain** How does Yosemite Valley show that ice changes Earth's surface?

3. **Explain** Describe how weathering, erosion, and deposition might change the valley during the next thousand years.

Volcanoes

Volcanic eruptions cause rapid changes in Earth's surface. Melted rock in the mantle, or magma, rises to Earth's surface. Expanding gases in the magma can cause an explosive eruption. Magma that erupts or flows onto Earth's surface is called lava. Hot ash and lava released during an eruption may quickly bury or destroy nearby forests and towns.

Ash from this eruption in Iceland covered hundreds of square kilometers. Volcanic ash is made up of tiny pieces of rock.

SUPPORTING STANDARD TEKS 3.7.B:
Investigate rapid changes in Earth's surface
such as volcanic eruptions, earthquakes,
and landslides.

In 2010, Iceland's Eyjafjallajökull (AY-uh-ful-ā-hō-kul) volcano erupted ash and hot gases several kilometers into the sky.

Science in a Snap!

Erupting Volcano

Make a model of an erupting volcano. Choose a place outdoors. Shake a bottle of seltzer water. Observe any bubbles of gas that form.

Hold the bottle pointing away from you and others. Open the cap and observe what happens to the gas and liquid in the bottle when the pressure is released.

How is this action like that of magma and gases erupting from a volcano?

WRAP IT UP !

1. **Recall**   What is magma?

2. **Explain**   How does a volcanic eruption cause rapid changes to Earth's surface?

SHAKE AND QUAKE

In areas of the world near a fault, the movement of Earth's plates can result in rapid changes to Earth's surface. One example of a rapid change is an earthquake. An earthquake usually occurs inside a fault, or boundary, where pressure has built up between slabs of rock. When the slabs of rock break free, the release of pressure causes a jolt. Shock waves quickly move out in all directions, and the ground shakes. Several million earthquakes occur every year. Most of them happen far from people or are too weak for people to notice.

On March 11, 2011, a powerful earthquake struck near Honshu, Japan. The earthquake rapidly changed Earth's surface, damaging roads, bridges, and buildings.

voCAB

tsunami
([t]sū-NAH-mē)

A **tsunami** is a series of ocean waves caused by an underwater earthquake or landslide.

SUPPORTING STANDARD TEKS 3.7.B:
Investigate rapid changes in Earth's surface such as volcanic eruptions, earthquakes, and landslides.

The March 11 earthquake was so powerful that it moved parts of northeastern Japan 2.4 meters (8 feet). A few minutes after the earthquake, a **tsunami** crashed over a seawall in Miyako City. Tsunamis up to 12 meters (39 feet) tall destroyed coastal areas across northeastern Japan.

My science notebook WRAP IT UP!

1. **Recall** What causes earthquakes?

2. **Explain** How can earthquakes cause rapid changes to Earth's surface?

3. **Predict** Suppose slabs of rock in a large fault have been locked together. The pressure is now very great. Describe the changes to Earth's surface that may occur when the slabs of rock break free.

SLIP AND SLIDE

Have you ever seen a road sign that says *Caution: Falling Rock?* Rock on a ledge or steep hill may suddenly break loose and fall. Often it's just a rock or two. But at other times, it's a landslide. A landslide is a rapid movement of rock, soil, and other material down a hill or mountain. A landslide can change Earth's surface. If enough material falls, the shape of the hill or mountain can be changed.

Erosion caused this landslide. The landslide changed Earth's surface. What do you think will eventually happen to the grass and trees on the slope?

SUPPORTING STANDARD TEKS 3.7.B: Investigate rapid changes in Earth's surface such as volcanic eruptions, earthquakes, and landslides.

What causes landslides? Sometimes heavy rains can loosen soil and rocks on slopes. Weathering, volcanoes, and earthquakes can also start the motion. But it is the force of gravity that suddenly pulls the rocks and other loosened material downhill.

In Sumatra, Indonesia, an earthquake triggered landslides that changed Earth's surface and destroyed several villages.

My science notebook

WRAP IT UP!

1. **Explain** How do landslides cause rapid changes to Earth's surface?

2. **Cause and Effect** What makes material in any landslide move downhill?

3. **Explain** How might an earthquake start a landslide?

85

Natural RESOURCES

Earth is full of the natural resources that people need. People need clean air to breathe and clean water to drink. People grow plants and raise animals for food. Air, water, plants, and animals are **renewable resources** that are continually being replaced. Use the photos on this page to learn more about some of Earth's renewable resources.

RENEWABLE RESOURCES

air

plants

water

animals

Air is a renewable resource. People need clean air to breathe.

Crops such as cotton can be replanted, year after year. New trees can be planted to replace those that people cut down.

People need clean fresh water to drink. Water can be cleaned and used again.

If people are mindful of how many fish they catch, enough fish will live to reproduce over and over.

voCAB

renewable resources
(rē-NŪ-uh-bul RĒ-sors-es)

Renewable resources are those that are always being replaced and will not run out.

nonrenewable resources
(non-rē-NŪ-uh-bul RĒ-sors-es)

Nonrenewable resources are those that cannot be replaced quickly enough to keep from running out.

fossil fuel
(FOS-ul FYŪ-ul)

A fossil fuel is a source of energy that formed from the remains of plants and animals that lived millions of years ago.

SUPPORTING STANDARD TEKS 4.7.C:
Identify and classify Earth's renewable resources, including air, plants, water, and animals; and nonrenewable resources, including coal, oil, and natural gas; and the importance of conservation.

Not all resources are renewable. **Nonrenewable resources** are those that cannot be replaced quickly enough to keep from running out. **Fossil fuels** are nonrenewable. Fossil fuels are sources of energy that formed slowly over time from the remains of plants and animals that lived millions of years ago. Use the photos on this page to learn more about some of Earth's nonrenewable resources.

NONRENEWABLE RESOURCES

coal

oil

natural gas

Coal formed slowly over time from plants that died millions of years ago. This resource will run out.

People use oil at a fast pace. People cannot replace the oil they use.

Natural gas is burned to heat water and warm homes. The natural gas that people use cannot be replaced.

My science notebook

WRAP IT UP!

1. **Classify** Are trees a renewable or nonrenewable resource? Explain your answer.

2. **Contrast** How do renewable and nonrenewable resources differ?

3. **Apply** List three ways you use renewable resources and three ways you use nonrenewable resources.

Practicing
CONSERVATION

When people talk about being "green," they're talking about **conservation.** Conservation is the careful use of natural resources. People need to protect and care for renewable resources.

Water is a renewable resource that living things need to survive. One way people can conserve water is to turn off the faucet when washing hands or brushing teeth. Plants are another renewable resource. Trees and other plants provide shelter for animals and restore oxygen to the air. People can help conserve forests by planting trees to replace those that are cut down.

When trees at this tree farm are cut down, farmers plant new trees like these to replace them.

voCAB

conservation
(kon-suhr-VĀ-shun)

Conservation is the protection and care of natural resources.

SUPPORTING STANDARD TEKS 4.7.C: Identify and classify Earth's renewable resources, including air, plants, water, and animals; and nonrenewable resources, including coal, oil, and natural gas; and the importance of conservation.

You can practice conservation by reducing your use of nonrenewable resources, too. Reducing use of fossil fuels, such as coal, oil, and natural gas, helps keep air clean. Reusing and recycling are other ways to conserve nonrenewable resources. Coal, oil, and natural gas are used to make things such as paper, glass bottles, and soda cans. You can put paper, glass, and aluminum cans in a recycling bin, not in the trash. Congratulations! You are greener already.

These items were made from recycled materials. The bag was made from old airplane seats. The bench was made from recycled plastic milk bottles.

WRAP IT UP!

My science notebook

1. **Recall**   How can you conserve renewable resources?

2. **Explain**   Why is it important to practice conservation?

3. **Apply**   Describe one way you can conserve water.

89

INVESTIGATE
SOIL PROPERTIES

 Which kind of soil can hold the most water?

Different types of soil can hold different amounts of water. The color of soil depends on minerals and other materials in the soil. The texture of soil can be described by observing the particle sizes and how the soil feels when it is moistened. In this investigation you can observe how much water different soils can hold. You can also observe the colors and textures of the soils.

MATERIALS

plastic cup

2 funnels

3 pieces of paper towel

spoon

sandy soil

clay soil

loam

graduated cylinder

water

hand lens

READY SET STAAR

SUPPORTING STANDARD TEKS 4.7.A:
Examine properties of soils, including color
and texture, capacity to retain water, and
ability to support the growth of plants.

1

Place a funnel in a plastic cup. Line the funnel with a piece of paper towel. Put 7 spoonfuls of sandy soil into the funnel.

2

Use a graduated cylinder to pour 75 mL of water onto the soil. Wait 10 minutes. Remove the funnel with the soil.

3

Use a funnel to pour the water from the cup into the graduated cylinder. Measure the amount of water that flowed through the soil. Record your data in your science notebook.

My science notebook

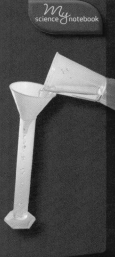

4

Use a hand lens to observe the color and size of particles of the soil in the funnel. To observe texture, rub a pinch of the moistened soil between your thumb and a finger. Record your observations. Repeat the steps using clay soil, then loam.

My science notebook

WRAP IT UP !

1. **Summarize** Which soil held the most water? Which soil held the least water?

2. **Contrast** How were the colors and textures of the soils different?

3. **Infer** Which soil do you think would be best for a garden? Why?

91

INVESTIGATE
SOIL AND
PLANTS

 Is sandy soil, clay soil, or loam best for growing corn?

Soil contains small pieces of rocks, minerals, water, and air. Bits of dead plants and animals, or humus, can also be found in soil. There are many types of soil. Sandy soil has larger particles than other soils and allows water to flow through easily. Clay soil has very small particles through which water flows slowly. Loam can contain humus and particles of different sizes. In this investigation, you can find out how well plants grow in three types of soil.

MATERIALS

sandy soil

clay soil

loam

hand lens

spoon

3 corn seedlings

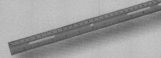
metric ruler

water

READY SET STAAR

SUPPORTING STANDARD TEKS 4.7.A:
Examine properties of soils, including color
and texture, capacity to retain water, and
ability to support the growth of plants.

1

Observe the properties of each type of soil. Use a hand lens to observe the color and size of the particles. Observe how each type of soil feels. Record your observations in your science notebook.

My science notebook

2

Predict which soil will be best for growing a corn seedling. Record your prediction.

3

Use a spoon to plant 1 corn seedling in each cup. Make sure only the roots are covered with soil. Then use a metric ruler to measure the height of each seedling. Record your data in a table.

4

Place the seedlings in a sunny place. Give each seedling 5 spoonfuls of water every day. After 1 week, measure the seedlings again. Record your data.

My science notebook

WRAP IT UP !

1. **Explain** Did your results support your prediction? Explain.

2. **Conclude** What can you conclude about which kind of soil is best for growing corn plants? Use your observations as evidence.

93

SEDIMENTARY ROCK

Sediments are tiny bits of rock, shells, sand, and other materials. Sediments settle on land or on the bottom of rivers, lakes, and oceans. New layers of sediment press down on old layers. Over many years, the sediments are pressed together. Some minerals act like cement and hold the sediments together. This process leads to the formation of sedimentary rock. Many sedimentary rocks have layers such as the ones shown here. Each layer represents a time when sediments were brought into the area and laid down.

Years of weathering and erosion have exposed colorful layers of sedimentary rock near Arizona's Paria River.

VOCAB

sedimentary rock
(sed-i-MEN-tah-rē ROK)

Many **sedimentary rocks** form from small pieces of rocks and minerals that are cemented together.

READINESS STANDARD TEKS 5.7.A:
Explore the processes that led to
the formation of sedimentary rocks
and fossil fuels.

Sandstone is one kind of sedimentary rock. The diagram below shows
the process that leads to the formation of sandstone. Layers of sand might
come from deserts, beaches, and the bottom of shallow seas. Over many
years, the layers of sand become squeezed together and form sandstone.

SAND INTO SANDSTONE

These sand dunes form
layers of sediment.

The lower layers are
squeezed together by the
weight of the upper layers.
Minerals between the
grains of sand hold the
sand together.

Over time, wind, water,
and ice uncover the
sandstone. You can see
where the separate layers
of sediment hardened.

My science notebook

WRAP IT UP!

1. **Describe**   What processes led to the formation of
   sandstone, a kind of sedimentary rock?

2. **Analyze**   Think about squeezing a fist-full of mud or
   wet sand. How is this like the process that leads to the
   formation of sedimentary rock? What else would be
   needed to form sedimentary rock?

INVESTIGATE
FOSSILS

? **How can you use a model to infer about past environments?**

Sedimentary rocks often contain fossils that give scientists clues to the past. In this investigation, you can make a model of a sedimentary rock containing fossils. First read the Fossil Environment chart below.

FOSSIL ENVIRONMENT

LAYER COLOR	ENVIRONMENT WHEN LAYER FORMED
Green	Dry land; warm temperatures
Yellow	Ice-covered land; dry, cold climate
Red	Warm, shallow ocean water; warm, humid climate
Tan	Cool, freshwater lake; warm temperatures

MATERIALS

 **4 lumps of clay**    **4 small objects**   **plastic knife**   **toothpick**    **craft stick**

SUPPORTING STANDARD TEKS 5.7.D:
Identify fossils as evidence of past living organisms and the nature of the environments at the time using models.

1

Flatten 1 lump of clay. This represents a layer of soil laid down millions of years ago. Press an object into the clay. The object represents an animal that died. Over time the soil formed rock. The animal became a fossil.

2

Add another layer of clay. This represents soil that covered the first layer and became rock. Press an object into this layer. Add 2 more layers with objects.

3

My science notebook

Exchange model rocks with another group. Cut through all of the layers. Draw the layers of the model in your science notebook.

4

Use a toothpick or craft stick to remove the model fossils. Draw each one in the layer in which it was found. Use the chart to learn about each organism's environment. Record the data on your drawing.

My science notebook **WRAP IT UP !**

1. **Conclude** Fossils of some sea animals would belong in the red layer of rock. Describe their environment.

2. **Infer** What can you infer about how the environment of the area where each fossil was found changed over the years?

97

FOSSIL FUELS

Coal, oil, and natural gas are fossil fuels. A fossil fuel is a source of energy that formed from the remains of plants and animals that lived millions of years ago. Coal formed from trees and giant ferns that died and fell into swamps. Mud piled on top, and the plant remains turned into a spongy material called peat. Over time, the peat was buried even deeper. As air and water were squeezed out, it slowly hardened into coal.

USE OF FOSSIL FUELS IN TEXAS

Coal, oil, and natural gas make up more than 90% of the total amount of energy that is used in Texas.

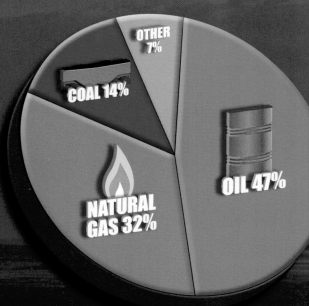

OTHER 7%

COAL 14%

OIL 47%

NATURAL GAS 32%

Oil rigs are built to remove oil and natural gas that are under the ocean floor.

READINESS STANDARD TEKS 5.7.A:
Explore the processes that led to the formation
of sedimentary rocks and fossil fuels.

Read the diagram below to see how plant and animal remains changed to oil and natural gas. Fossil fuels, such as oil and natural gas, formed from dead plants and animals that sank to the ocean floor millions of years ago. The plant and animal remains first had to be buried under many layers of mud and rock. The weight of the layers above produced pressure and heat. Gradually, this pressure and heat caused the remains to change into oil or natural gas.

OIL AND NATURAL GAS FORMATION

ocean

dead organisms buried under sediment

oil forming

oil rig

oil

natural gas

My science notebook **WRAP IT UP !**

1. **Compare and Contrast** How is the process by which fossil fuels form similar to the process by which sedimentary rocks form? How is it different?

2. **Explain** Why don't fossil fuels look like plants or animals?

CONSERVING FOSSIL FUELS

This airport in Texas depends on energy. Without energy from electricity, airports would not have runway lights. The buildings would be dark, too. Most of this electricity comes from burning coal or natural gas. The engines that power airplanes, cars, trucks, and buses also depend on energy. Most burn fuel to get from one place to another.

The Dallas/Fort Worth International Airport uses different forms of energy to function. Most of this energy comes from fossil fuels.

SUPPORTING STANDARD TEKS 4.7.C:
Identify and classify Earth's renewable resources, including air, plants, water, and animals; and nonrenewable resources, including coal, oil, and natural gas; and the importance of conservation.

In the United States today, most fuels are made from oil. The chart below shows how much oil the United States and some other countries use every day. Fossil fuels are nonrenewable. People can practice conservation by using less coal, natural gas, and oil. Conserving fossil fuels will help them last longer. But one day, Earth's supply of fossil fuels will run out. People will need other energy resources in the future.

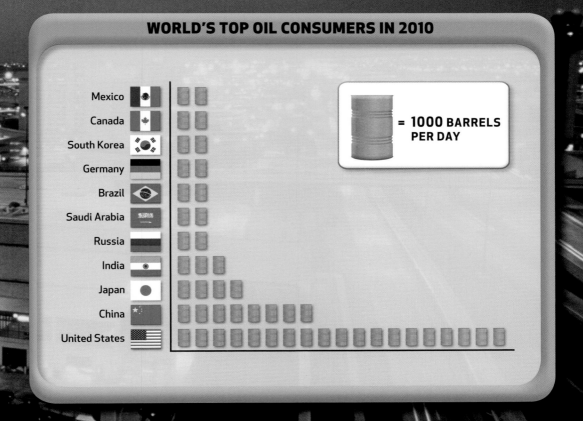

WORLD'S TOP OIL CONSUMERS IN 2010

= 1000 BARRELS PER DAY

WRAP IT UP!

My science notebook

1. **Interpret Charts** Which countries consumed more than 2,000 barrels of oil per day in 2010?

2. **Evaluate** Why is conserving fossil fuels important?

101

WIND ENERGY

In the future, more and more of the energy people use may come from resources other than fossil fuels. These are called **alternative energy resources.** Wind is one alternative energy resource. It is a clean, renewable resource. In windy locations, the energy in wind can be used to make electricity. Wind power plants contain many wind turbines. A wind turbine has wing-like blades. The wind spins the blades of the turbine. This runs a generator, a machine that makes the electricity.

Turbines at a wind power plant near Abilene, Texas

voCAB

alternative energy resource
(awl-TUR-nuh-tiv EN-ur-jē RĒ-sors)

An **alternative energy resource** is a source of energy that can be used in place of fossil fuels.

READINESS STANDARD TEKS 5.7.C:
Identify alternative energy resources such as wind, solar, hydroelectric, geothermal, and biofuels.

Most wind turbines are tall to catch the strong, steady winds high above the ground. Some of the electricity that you use may come from wind energy. Look at the map. Texas produces more wind energy than any other state.

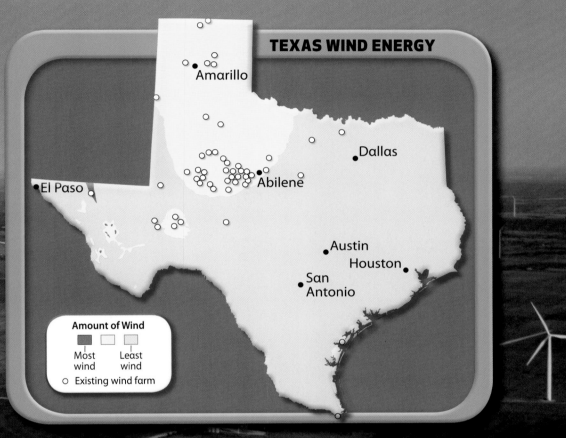

TEXAS WIND ENERGY

Amarillo

Dallas

El Paso

Abilene

Austin

Houston

San Antonio

Amount of Wind

Most wind | Least wind

○ Existing wind farm

My science notebook

WRAP IT UP !

1. **Identify** Why is wind called an alternative energy resource?

2. **Interpret Maps** Describe the connection you see between amount of wind and the locations of most of the wind farms.

3. **Infer** Can more electricity be made at wind power plants on calm days or windy days? Explain.

103

SOLAR ENERGY

Sunlight is a clean, renewable source of energy. Solar energy, or energy from the Sun, is an alternative energy resource. How does solar energy work? Think about a solar calculator. It contains tiny solar cells. Solar cells use light to make electricity. What if you wanted to power a whole house, or even a city? For more power, solar panels are used. The panels contain thousands of solar cells.

This car doesn't need to stop for gas. It has solar cells that change sunlight to electricity. The electricity powers the car's engine.

READINESS STANDARD TEKS 5.7.C:
Identify alternative energy resources such as wind, solar, hydroelectric, geothermal, and biofuels.

Some solar power plants use hundreds of curved mirrors that direct or focus sunlight onto a small surface. The energy from sunlight causes water to heat up and change to steam. The steam turns the blades of a turbine. The turbine then runs a generator that produces electricity. Producing electricity from sunlight is an alternative to burning coal or natural gas.

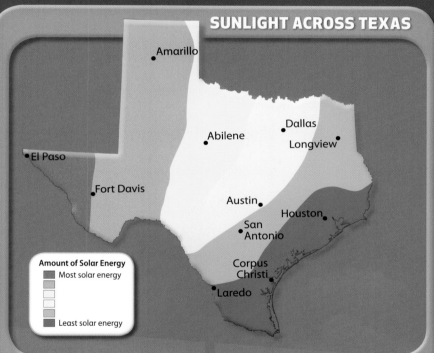

SUNLIGHT ACROSS TEXAS

Amarillo

Dallas
Abilene
Longview

El Paso

Fort Davis

Austin
Houston
San
Antonio

Corpus
Christi
Laredo

Amount of Solar Energy
Most solar energy

Least solar energy

Sunlight bounces off of these mirrors and heats water to make steam. The steam generates electrical energy.

The map shows the intensity, or directness, of sunlight across the state. The greater the intensity of sunlight, the more solar energy can be produced.

My science notebook **WRAP IT UP!**

1. **Identify** Why is solar energy called an alternative energy resource?

2. **Compare** How are solar energy and wind energy alike?

3. **Apply** Which city is located in the area with the highest potential to produce electricity from solar energy? Explain.

HYDROELECTRIC ENERGY

Have you ever stepped into a stream and felt the water tugging at your feet? Moving water has energy. **Hydroelectric power** is electricity that is made by using the energy of moving water. Hydroelectric power is an alternative energy resource because fossil fuels are not needed to produce the electricity.

The Grand Coulee Dam is the biggest hydroelectric dam in the United States. It changes the movement of water into energy that people can use.

voCAB

hydroelectric power
(hī-drō-i-LEK-trik POW-ur)

Hydroelectric power is electricity produced by the energy in moving water.

READINESS STANDARD TEKS 5.7.C:
Identify alternative energy resources such as wind, solar, hydroelectric, geothermal, and biofuels.

A dam can be built on a river to produce electricity. The dam holds back some of the water. This forms a lake. Study the diagram to understand how electricity is made at a hydroelectric power plant. This electricity travels through wires to homes and businesses.

HYDROELECTRIC POWER PLANT

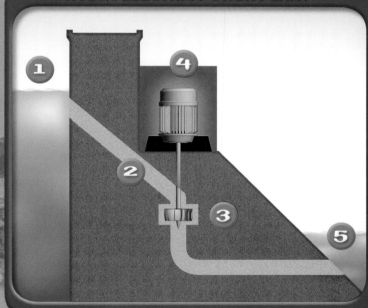

1. Water from the lake enters the hydroelectric plant.

2. Passages that can be opened and closed guide water through the plant at high speed.

3. The force of the water causes turbines to move.

4. Generators attached to the turbines change the energy from the moving water to electrical energy.

5. The water continues moving down the river.

My science notebook

WRAP IT UP!

1. **Identify** Why is hydroelectric energy called an alternative energy resource?

2. **Cause and Effect** What causes the turbines to move in a hydroelectric power plant?

3. **Explain** How does a hydroelectric power plant produce electricity?

GEOTHERMAL ENERGY

Geothermal energy is an alternative energy resource. Geothermal energy is heat energy from within Earth. This heat energy melts rock. In some places, the hot, melted rock is close to Earth's surface. Geothermal power plants can be built at these locations.

In geothermal power plants, the hot rock heats water, forming steam. The steam is forced out of the ground. Energy from the steam turns turbines. The turbines run generators that produce electricity.

At this geothermal power plant in Iceland, what looks like smoke is actually tiny droplets of water.

voCAB

geothermal energy
(jē-ō-THER-mul EN-ur-jē)

Geothermal energy is heat energy from within Earth.

READINESS STANDARD TEKS 5.7.C:
Identify alternative energy resources such as wind, solar, hydroelectric, geothermal, and biofuels.

The western states have the most geothermal resources in the United States. The map shows areas of Texas that could best make use of this alternative energy resource.

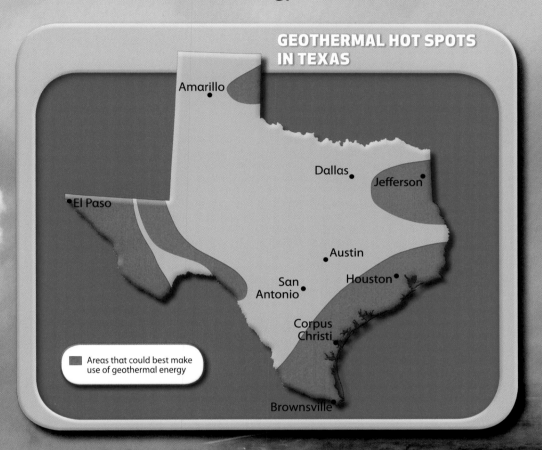

GEOTHERMAL HOT SPOTS IN TEXAS

Amarillo

Dallas

Jefferson

El Paso

Austin

Houston

San Antonio

Corpus Christi

Areas that could best make use of geothermal energy

Brownsville

My science notebook

WRAP IT UP!

1. **Identify** What alternative energy resource can use heat energy from within Earth to produce electricity?

2. **Contrast** How is geothermal energy different from energy that comes from fossil fuels?

3. **Infer** Why does melted rock need to be close to Earth's surface for a geothermal power plant to work well?

BIOFUELS

Biomass is a renewable resource that comes from plant material, such as paper and food products, or animal waste. Biomass has energy stored from plants and animals. Biofuels are an alternative energy resource made from biomass. Some kinds of biofuels can be used in generators to produce electricity.

Corn can be made into biofuels. Biofuels can be used to produce electricity and power some cars and trucks.

VOCAB

biofuel
(BĪ-ō-fyū-ul)

A **biofuel** is any fuel made from plant material or animal waste.

READINESS STANDARD TEKS 5.7.C:
Identify alternative energy resources such as wind, solar, hydroelectric, geothermal, and biofuels.

Ethanol is a biofuel that can be made from corn or other crops. Biodiesel fuel is made from plant and animal oils—even oil left over from making french fries. Ethanol and biodiesel can be used to run cars and trucks. These fuels are alternatives to fossil fuels.

Biodiesel fuel and ethanol in gasoline are available at many filling stations.

WRAP IT UP!

My science notebook

1. **Identify** Why are biofuels considered an alternative energy resource?

2. **Identify** What are three ways biofuels are used?

3. **Contrast** How are biofuels different from fossil fuels?

111

EVALUATING ENERGY RESOURCES

Scientists today are working on developing alternatives to fossil fuels such as wind, solar, hydroelectric, geothermal, and biofuel energy resources. These are all renewable resources and they are cleaner than fossil fuels. Still, no option is perfect. The chart on the next page gives you some of the advantages and disadvantages of each alternative energy resource.

On the Danish island of Samso, almost no fossil fuels are burned. People meet all of their energy needs using wind, solar, and biofuel resources.

READINESS STANDARD TEKS 5.7.C:
Identify alternative energy resources such as wind, solar, hydroelectric, geothermal, and biofuels.

ADVANTAGES	**DISADVANTAGES**

WIND

- Renewable: won't run out
- No pollution

- Wind not always blowing
- Can be noisy
- May harm birds

SOLAR

- Renewable: won't run out
- No pollution

- Less sunlight on cloudy days
- Takes up a lot of space
- Costly

HYDROELECTRIC

- Renewable: won't run out
- Low pollution
- Reliable

- Can destroy habitats
- Costly

GEOTHERMAL

- Renewable: won't run out
- Little or no pollution

- Not available in most areas
- Costly

BIOFUEL

- Renewable: won't run out
- Low pollution
- Can come from garbage

- Farmland used for fuel crops rather than food crops
- Cannot be used in all cars and trucks

My science notebook

WRAP IT UP!

1. **Identify** Name five alternative energy resources.

2. **Compare and Contrast** Choose two alternative energy resources. Tell how they are alike and different.

WEATHER

When you get ready to go outside, you probably check the **weather** to see if it is sunny or cloudy, hot or cold. Weather is the state of the atmosphere at a certain place and time. All weather occurs in the atmosphere. The atmosphere is a layer of gases that wraps around Earth like a blanket.

partly cloudy

The weather is partly cloudy. The amount of cloud cover can change throughout the day.

foggy

The weather is foggy and cool. Fog is a cloud that forms near the ground.

voCAB

weather
(WE-thur)

Weather is the state of the atmosphere at a certain place and time.

The weather is cloudy and humid. Dark storm clouds bring rain and lightning.

Weather changes from season to season. It changes from day to day. Weather can even change from hour to hour. The sky might be bright and sunny in the morning but turn rainy by afternoon. You can observe and describe weather by measuring properties of the air such as temperature, wind speed, and humidity. Humidity is the amount of water vapor that air can hold.

sunny

The weather on this day is sunny and warm. It's a perfect time to be outside.

My science notebook WRAP IT UP!

1. **Define** What is weather?

2. **List** Name three properties of air that can be measured to describe weather.

3. **Apply** Describe the weather where you live on a usual winter or summer day. Use some of the properties of weather in your description.

CLIMATE

When people say, "It is hot here in the summer," they are talking about the **climate** of a particular place. Climate is the pattern of weather of an area over a long period of time.

Look at the map of climate zones in Texas. The range of temperatures and the amount of precipitation in an area determine its climate. Each type of climate has certain weather patterns that are the same or repeated year after year.

voCAB

climate
(KLĪ-mit)

Climate is the pattern of weather of an area over a long period of time.

READY SET STAAR

SUPPORTING STANDARD TEKS 5.8.A:
Differentiate between weather and climate.

Palo Duro Canyon State Park is in a part of Texas that has a mixed-dry climate. Mixed-dry climates are cooler on average than hot climates and get less precipitation than humid climates.

CLIMATE ZONES IN TEXAS

mixed-dry

mixed-humid

hot-dry

hot-humid

These cotton fields in Fisher County grow in a part of Texas that has a mixed-humid climate. Summers are warm, but winters are cool. More than 50 cm (20 in) of precipitation falls per year.

The eastern part of Texas has a hot-humid climate. Summers are hot and humid. Winters are mild. More than 114 cm (45 in) of precipitation falls per year.

Guadalupe Mountains National Park is in a part of Texas that has a hot-dry climate. The average temperature stays well above freezing, even in winter months. This region in Texas gets the least amount of precipitation.

My science notebook

WRAP IT UP!

1. **Contrast** What is the difference between weather and climate?

2. **Compare** How are hot-humid and mixed-humid climates alike?

3. **Interpret Maps** Look at the climate map. Which area of Texas receives more precipitation, Guadalupe Mountains National Park or eastern Texas?

117

On this Monday morning in San Francisco, the **weather** is foggy. The air is damp and cool. Later in the day, the air temperature increases and the fog clears.

Monday

Tuesday

The weather is sunny and clear all day on Tuesday. The temperature on this day is warmer. The air feels dry.

On Wednesday afternoon, clouds hide part of the Sun. The weather is warm and breezy. The humidity increases during the day. The air feels sticky.

Wednesday

Thursday

Thursday morning brings rain and clouds. By evening the sky begins to clear. The temperature drops at night.

voCAB

weather
(WE-thur)

Weather is the state of the atmosphere at a

CLIMATE

Marine **climates** in California have dry summers and wet winters. Ocean currents contribute to mild temperatures along the coast.

Winters in high mountain areas are cold. Some summer days can be hot.

cold

mixed-dry

marine

Mixed-dry climates get less than 50 cm (20 in) of precipitation per year.

hot-dry

Joshua Tree National Park is in a part of California that has a hot-dry climate. Less than 12 cm (5 in) of precipitation falls per year.

SHARE AND COMPARE

- Write about how the weather in San Francisco can change from day to day and how the climate in California changes from region to region.

- Share your information with another group. Compare the climate and weather that the other group wrote about.

- Explain how weather and climate are different.

VOCAB

climate
(KLĪ-mit)

Climate is the pattern of weather of an area over a long period of time.

119

WEATHER maps

Suppose you want to predict what the weather will be like two days from now. You might look at a weather map. Symbols on a weather map show where fronts are moving. A front is the area where two different air masses meet. Weather events, such as thunderstorms and blizzards, happen at fronts. These maps show the weather in Texas on three days.

DAY 1

WEATHER MAP KEY

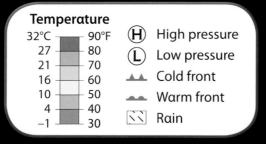

Temperature			
32°C	90°F	(H)	High pressure
27	80	(L)	Low pressure
21	70	▲▲▲	Cold front
16	60	● ●	Warm front
10	50		
4	40	⟍⟍	Rain
−1	30		

ZZZAP!

Worldwide, about 100 bolts of lightning strike Earth's surface every second! A bolt of lightning may be as much as five times hotter than the surface of the Sun.

SUPPORTING STANDARD TEKS 4.8.A: Measure and record changes in weather and make predictions using weather maps, weather symbols, and a map key.

Symbols on a weather map also show areas of high and low air pressure. High air pressure often brings clear skies. Low air pressure often brings clouds and rain. Wind is the movement of air from areas of high pressure to areas of low pressure.

DAY 2

DAY 3

My science notebook

WRAP IT UP!

1. **Interpret Maps** Find where your city or town is on the weather maps. Look at the symbols. Describe the weather on each of the three days.

2. **Predict** Use the maps and map key to predict what the weather will be like in your city or town on the fourth day.

121

INVESTIGATE WEATHER

 How can you measure changes in air pressure?

Scientists collect data about the atmosphere to identify weather patterns. Weather data from thousands of sources help scientists make predictions. In this investigation, you can make a barometer to measure changes in air pressure. Then you can look for patterns in air pressure and weather conditions.

MATERIALS

cut balloon

plastic cup

rubber band

glue stick

straw

metric ruler

SUPPORTING STANDARD TEKS 4.8.A: Measure and record changes in weather and make predictions using weather maps, weather symbols, and a map key.

1

Stretch a cut balloon over the top of a plastic cup. Use a rubber band to secure the balloon tightly around the cup. Glue a straw halfway across the balloon surface.

2

Place your barometer on a flat surface. Use a metric ruler to measure the height of the straw in mm. Record the data in your science notebook.

3

Measure the height of the tip of the straw each day for a week. On days of high air pressure, the balloon will sink down and the tip of the straw will be higher. On days of low air pressure, the balloon will bulge out and the tip of the straw will be lower.

4

Record your observations of cloud cover and precipitation for each day. Combine the data onto a calendar. Look for patterns in your data.

WRAP IT UP!

1. **Explain** How did the data for air pressure measurements vary during the week?

2. **Analyze** Describe any patterns you find in air pressure measurements and weather conditions.

123

THE WATER CYCLE

The movement of water from Earth to the air and back to Earth is called the **water cycle.** The water cycle repeats over and over again. Read the diagram to learn about the water cycle.

When the Sun shines on Earth's water, heat energy causes the liquid water to evaporate into water vapor, a gas. The water vapor rises into the air. Most of Earth's water is in the ocean.

Evaporation

Groundwater and Runoff

voCAB

water cycle
(WAH-tur SĪ-kul)

The **water cycle** is the movement of water from Earth's surface to the air and back again.

Some water that does not evaporate soaks through the ground and becomes groundwater. Other water flows over Earth's surface as runoff.

SUPPORTING STANDARD TEKS 5.8.B:
Explain how the Sun and the ocean interact
in the water cycle.

SUPPORTING STANDARD TEKS 4.8.B:
Describe and illustrate the continuous
movement of water above and on the
surface of Earth through the water cycle
and explain the role of the Sun as a major
source of energy in this process.

Earth's surface holds a limited supply of water. Most of that water is in the ocean. The water is always being recycled. Energy from the Sun continuously moves water through the water cycle.

Condensation

As water vapor rises, it cools and condenses, or changes from a gas to a liquid. Water vapor condenses into tiny drops of water that form clouds.

Precipitation

Ocean waves break along the coast of South Padre Island in Texas. How will the Sun's energy affect the water in the ocean?

My science notebook

WRAP IT UP!

1. **Summarize** Draw and label a diagram of the water cycle. Explain how the Sun interacts with the ocean and other water on Earth's surface in the water cycle.

2. **Explain** Tell how water from a river or lake may have once been in the ocean.

Water falls as precipitation from clouds. It may reach the surface as rain, freezing rain, sleet, snow, or hail.

THE SOLAR SYSTEM

The solar system includes the Sun and all of the objects that **revolve,** or move around, the Sun. The planets in order of their distance from the Sun are Mercury, Venus, Earth, Mars, Jupiter, Saturn, Uranus, and Neptune. The eight planets are the largest objects that revolve around the Sun. Each planet's path around the Sun is called its **orbit.** The diagram shows the planets and their orbits around the Sun.

Sun

Mercury

Venus

Earth

Mars

Jupiter

VOCAB

revolve
(re-VAWLV)

To **revolve** is to travel around another object in space.

orbit
(ŌR-bit)

An **orbit** is the path Earth or another object takes in space as it revolves.

READY
SET
STAAR

SUPPORTING STANDARD TEKS 3.8.D:
Identify the planets in Earth's solar system
and their position in relation to the Sun.

A year is the length of time it takes a planet to complete its orbit around the Sun. The length of a year differs from planet to planet. A year on Earth is about 365 days. At only 88 Earth days, Mercury has the shortest year. Which planet do you think has the longest year?

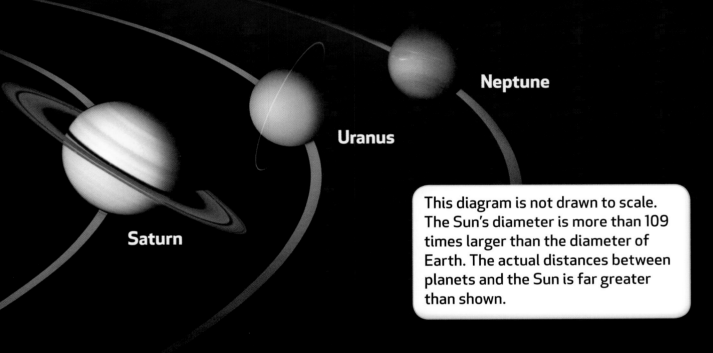

Neptune

Uranus

Saturn

This diagram is not drawn to scale. The Sun's diameter is more than 109 times larger than the diameter of Earth. The actual distances between planets and the Sun is far greater than shown.

My science *notebook*

WRAP IT UP !

1. **Identify** Name the planets in Earth's solar system and their position in relation to the Sun.

2. **Interpret** Look at the diagram of the solar system. How many planets are closer to the Sun than Earth? How many are farther away?

3. **Conclude** Based on the diagram, does Neptune or Saturn have a longer orbit? How can you tell?

127

COMPARING THE SUN, EARTH, AND MOON

What do you see when you look at the sky? By day or night, you might see the Moon in one shape or another. During the day, the Sun lights up the sky.

The Sun is huge compared to Earth and the Moon. If the Sun were the size of a basketball, look how small Earth would be. The Moon would be about the size of the period at the end of this sentence.

← **Size of the Sun**

← **Size of Earth**

The Moon can be seen in the sky sometimes at night and other times during the day.

SUPPORTING STANDARD TEKS 5.8.D:
Identify and compare the physical
characteristics of the Sun, Earth, and Moon.

Distances between Earth, the Moon, and the Sun are vast. If you were in a race car traveling at 160 kilometers per hour (about 100 miles per hour), it would take you 100 days to reach the Moon. It would take you about 106 years to travel to the Sun.

SUN

Structure:
Ball of hot gases

Surface:
Hot gases; no life

Diameter:
1,391,980 km
(about 856,000 mi.)

Distance from Earth:
149,597,892 km
(about 93,000,000 mi.)

Age:
4.55 billion years

EARTH

Structure:
Solid and liquid rock

Surface:
Rock and water;
layer of air; has life

Diameter:
12,742 km
(about 7,900 mi.)

Age:
4.54 billion years

MOON

Structure:
Solid and liquid rock

Surface:
Rock and dust; trace
of ice; no air; no life

Diameter:
3,476 km (2,160 mi.)

Distance from Earth:
384,400 km (about
238,000 mi.)

Age:
4.5 billion years

My science notebook **WRAP IT UP!**

1. **Identify** What are the physical characteristics of the Sun, Earth, and Moon?

2. **Compare and Contrast** How are the surfaces of the Sun, Earth, and Moon alike and different?

129

DAY AND NIGHT

Think about what happens when you **rotate,** or spin around. As you turn, you face different directions and see different things. Places on Earth are like that. Earth does not stand still. It rotates on an imaginary line called an **axis** that runs through the North and South poles.

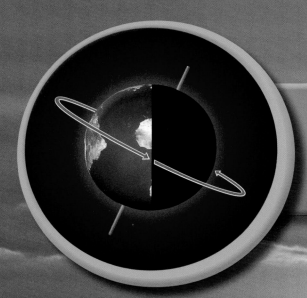

In about 24 hours, an area on the surface of Earth rotates into sunlight, then into darkness, and then back into sunlight.

voCAB

rotate
(RŌ-tāt)

To **rotate** is to spin around.

axis
(AK-sis)

An **axis** is an imaginary line around which Earth spins.

READINESS STANDARD TEKS 5.8.C:
Demonstrate that Earth rotates on its axis once approximately every 24 hours causing the day/night cycle and the apparent movement of the Sun across the sky.

Half of Earth always faces the Sun and is lit by sunlight. There it is day. The other half of Earth faces away from the Sun and is dark. There it is night. Earth makes one complete rotation approximately every 24 hours. That's why one complete day-night cycle lasts 24 hours.

Science in a Snap!   Night and Day

Mark your location on a globe with a piece of masking tape. Use a flashlight to represent the Sun. Shine it on the globe so that it is day where you live.

Rotate the globe so that it is night where you live.

? **What happened to the place on the globe where it used to be day? How often does this change happen?**

My science *notebook*   **WRAP IT UP!**

1. **Cause and Effect** How does Earth's rotation on its axis cause day and night?

2. **Apply** Which time period is closer to the scientific meaning of a day—the time period between sunrise and sunset or the 24-hour time period between one sunrise and the next sunrise?

MOVEMENT

Have you ever been on a merry-go-round? The people and objects on the ground seem to go by you, instead of the other way around. What you see is their **apparent movement.** Apparent movement is the way something appears to move even when it is not actually moving.

VOCAB

apparent movement
(uh-PAIR-ent MOOV-ment)

An object's **apparent movement** is the way it appears to move, not whether or how it actually moves.

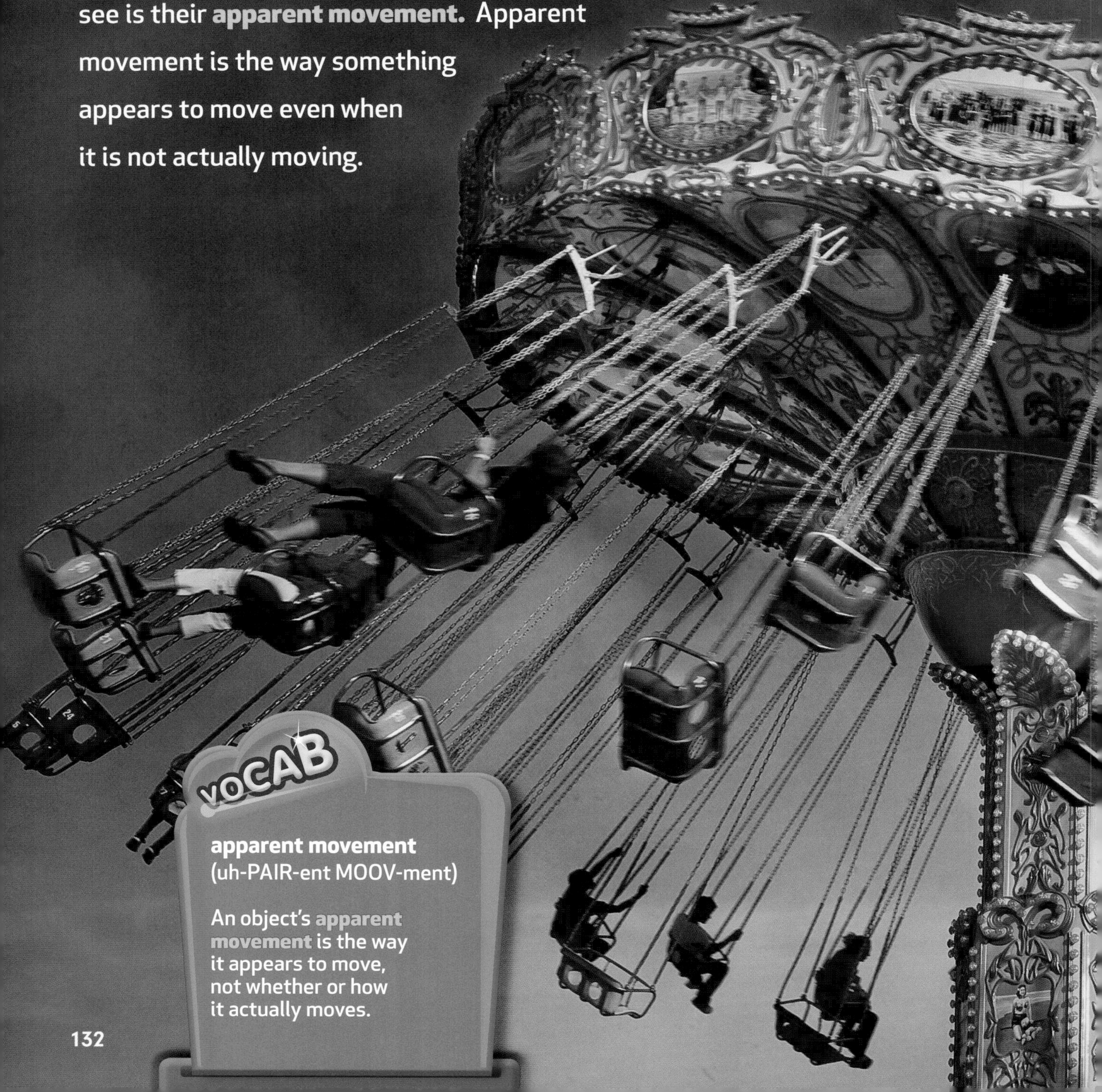

READINESS STANDARD TEKS 5.8.C: Demonstrate that Earth rotates on its axis once approximately every 24 hours causing the day/night cycle and the apparent movement of the Sun across the sky.

Earth's rotation is like that of a merry-go-round. Because Earth is so large, you don't sense its rotation. You feel as if you are staying still and everything else is moving. As Earth rotates on its axis, the Sun appears to move across the sky. But Earth — and you — are moving, not the Sun.

Science in a Snap!

Observe Apparent Movement

Choose a place outdoors. Note the location so you can return to the same spot. Draw a landmark that you observe when facing South. Label East and West. Observe where the Sun appears. Draw the Sun and record the time.

Every two hours, return to the same location. Repeat your observation. Describe how the Sun appears to move in the sky during the day.

? **What causes this pattern?**

WRAP IT UP!

1. **Cause and Effect** What causes the apparent movement of the Sun across the sky?

2. **Identify** When you see an airplane moving across the sky, are you observing apparent movement? Explain.

3. **Infer** Think about a time when you saw the moon and stars. Why do the Moon and stars appear to move in the sky?

INVESTIGATE
SUNLIGHT AND SHADOWS

 How does a shadow in sunlight change during the day?

At dawn, your location on Earth's surface moves out of darkness and into sunlight. As Earth rotates, the Sun appears to move across the sky. Shadows shorten and lengthen again. In this investigation, you can observe how the changing angle between the Sun and your location on Earth's surface affects shadows caused by sunlight.

clay

poster board

pencil

colored pencil

meterstick

READY SET STAAR

SUPPORTING STANDARD TEKS 4.8.C:
Collect and analyze data to identify
sequences and predict patterns of change in
shadows, tides, seasons, and the observable
appearance of the Moon over time.

1

Put poster board in a sunny place.
Put a clay ball on the poster board.
Push the end of a pencil into the clay.

2

Mark an **X** to show the direction of
the Sun. Record how high the Sun
looks in the sky. Trace the pencil's
shadow. Write the date and time
next to the shadow outline and
the X.

March 23
10:00AM
X

March 23
10:00AM

3

My science notebook

Use a meterstick to measure the
shadow. Record the measurement
and the time in your science
notebook. Then repeat steps
2 and 3 at three more times
during the day.

4

Use a colored pencil to draw where
you predict the shadow will be in
1 hour. After 1 hour, repeat steps
2 and 3 one more time.

My science notebook

WRAP IT UP !

1. **Identify** What patterns in length and movement did you observe
   with the shadows?

2. **Explain** Did your results support your prediction? How is the
   Sun's position related to the position and length of shadows?

THE PATTERN OF SEASONS

Weather in many places changes with the seasons. In some places, you might see colorful leaves on cool fall days. In many areas, winter can be cold and snowy. There are fewer daylight hours than in fall. In spring, days can be warmer and new leaves grow on some trees. Summer often brings warm or hot weather. Summer has more hours of daylight than spring.

The seasons repeat in the same pattern every year. The table on the next page has data collected through the seasons in Charlottesville, Virginia. Look for patterns in weather and length of daylight through the four seasons. What are the seasons like where you live?

winter — Snow falls on some winter days. Winter brings the least amount of precipitation.

spring — On some trees, flowers and new leaves grow as average temperatures and length of daylight increase in spring.

summer — Summer is the hottest season of the year in the Blue Ridge Mountains. It is also the season with the most precipitation.

SUPPORTING STANDARD TEKS 4.8.C:
Collect and analyze data to identify
sequences and predict patterns of change in
shadows, tides, seasons, and the observable
appearance of the Moon over time.

SEASONAL PATTERNS IN CHARLOTTESVILLE, VIRGINIA

	WINTER (Dec. 22–Mar. 19)	SPRING (Mar. 20–June 20)	SUMMER (June 21–Sept. 21)	FALL (Sept. 22–Dec. 21)
AVERAGE HIGH TEMPERATURE	9°C (48°F)	21°C (70°F)	28.5°C (83°F)	16°C (61°F)
AVERAGE LOW TEMPERATURE	–1°C (30°F)	9.5°C (49°F)	17°C (63°F)	5°C (41°F)
AVERAGE LENGTH OF DAYLIGHT	10 h 25 min	13 h 30 min	13 h 55 min	10 h 45 min
AVERAGE PRECIPITATION	20.68 cm (8.14 in)	27.42 cm (10.80 in)	33.78 cm (13.80 in)	26.24 cm (10.33 in)

fall

It is fall in the Blue
Ridge Mountains near
Charlottesville, Virginia.

In fall, there are fewer hours
of daylight and average
temperatures decrease.
The leaves of many trees
change color.

My science notebook WRAP IT UP !

1. **Sequence**   In what order do the seasons occur?

2. **Predict**   Use the table. Read the average length
   of daylight in each season. About how many hours
   of daylight will there be the following spring?

3. **Analyze**   Study the data in the table. Which two
   seasons are the most different from each other in
   temperature and precipitation?

TIDES

Tides are the cycle of rising and falling water levels around the world. They are caused by the pull of the Moon's gravity. You know that Earth's gravity keeps the Moon in orbit. But the Moon's gravity also affects Earth. Its gravity pulls on Earth's water, causing the ocean to bulge out. The bulges produce tides. In most places, high tide and low tide each happen twice a day. Compare high tide with low tide in Canada's Bay of Fundy.

BAY OF FUNDY TIDES

MONDAY		TUESDAY		WEDNESDAY	
Time	Height	Time	Height	Time	Height
3:39 AM	3.6 m	4:33 AM	3.3 m	5:21 AM	2.9 m
9:22 AM	9.8 m	10:14 AM	10.2 m	11:01 AM	10.7 m
3:59 PM	3.8 m	4:51 PM	3.5 m	5:38 PM	3.0 m
9:43 PM	10.5 m	10:33 PM	10.9 m	11:20 PM	11.4 m

It is high tide in Canada's Bay of Fundy. The tides here are extreme.

SUPPORTING STANDARD TEKS 4.8.C:
Collect and analyze data to identify
sequences and predict patterns of change in
shadows, tides, seasons, and the observable
appearance of the Moon over time.

A high tide happens in the area facing the Moon because the Moon's gravity pulls on Earth's water. A high tide also happens in the area facing away from the Moon. The Moon's gravity pulls Earth toward the Moon, leaving a bulge of water. Low tide happens everywhere else.

low tide

My science notebook **WRAP IT UP !**

1. **Sequence** Tell how the tides change during a 24-hour period.

2. **Predict** Use the data in the table to predict when the next high tide will occur on Thursday.

3. **Analyze** Use the tide table. Plot the tides on a graph for the three days.

139

INVESTIGATE
MOON PHASES

 How does the appearance of the Moon seem to change over time?

The phases you see from Earth result from the Moon's position in its orbit around Earth. In this investigation, you can observe a model to learn how the appearance of the lighted part of the moon changes.

MOON PHASES CALENDAR

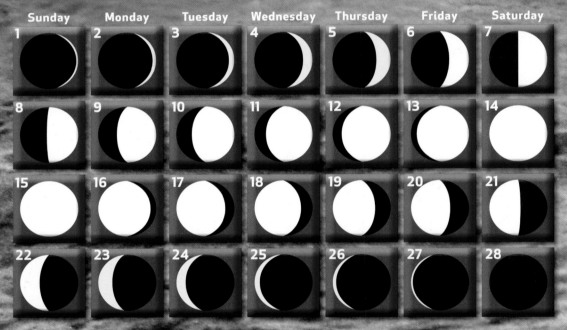

MATERIALS

| lamp | ball | craft stick | meterstick |

SUPPORTING STANDARD TEKS 4.8.C:
Collect and analyze data to identify sequences and predict patterns of change in shadows, tides, seasons, and the observable appearance of the Moon over time.

1 Push a craft stick into a foam ball. The ball is a model of the Moon. Place a lamp at eye level. The lamp represents the Sun. Stand 2 meters from the lamp and hold the craft stick. You represent Earth.

2 Have a partner stand near the lamp. Have a second partner stand behind you. Raise the ball slightly above your head.

3 *My science notebook*

Turn your body in a circle. Observe the light on the ball as you turn. Have your partners observe the ball. Record all observations in your science notebook.

4 Look at the Moon Phases Calendar. Make a plan with your partners to show the same pattern of Moon phases using the Moon model. Try your plan.

My science notebook

WRAP IT UP !

1. **Sequence** In step 4, did you move in a clockwise or in a counterclockwise direction to produce the phases of the Moon in the observable sequence that matches the Moon data on page 140?

2. **Predict** What pattern will you observe if you continue turning in the same direction?

REVOLVE

The Moon **revolves** around Earth and travels with Earth around the Sun. A year on Earth is about 365 days— the length of time it takes Earth to complete its **orbit**.

THE PATTERN OF SEASONS

As Earth revolves, the four seasons are a pattern that repeats every year.

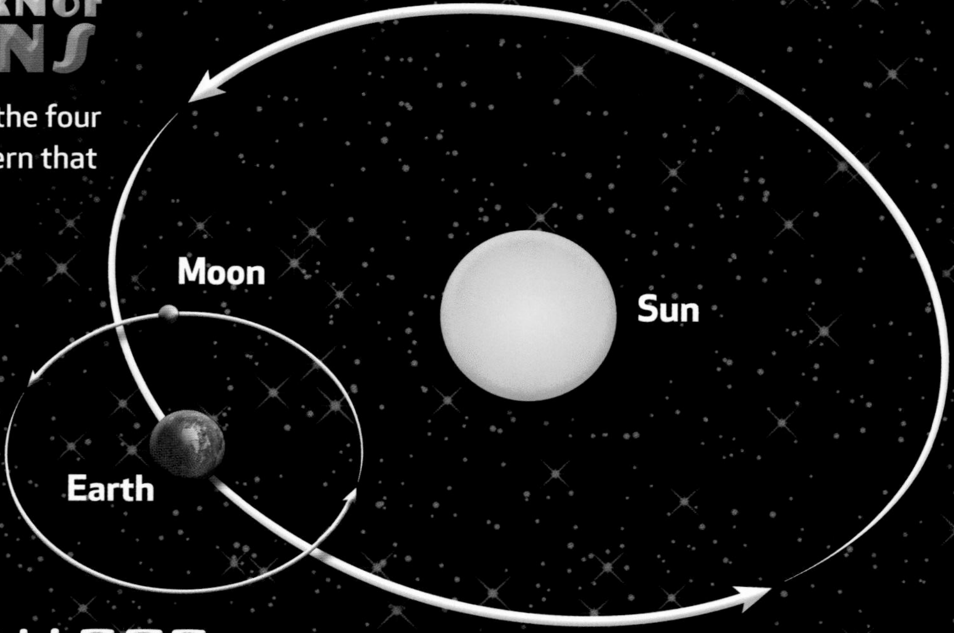

Moon

Sun

Earth

MOON PHASES

The Sun shines on the half of the Moon that is facing it. As the Moon slowly revolves around Earth, you see changing amounts of this lighted half.

voCAB

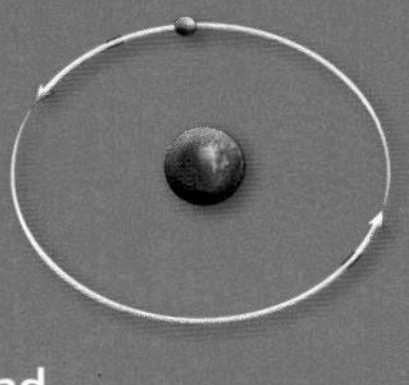

revolve
(re-VAWLV)

To **revolve** is to travel around another object in space.

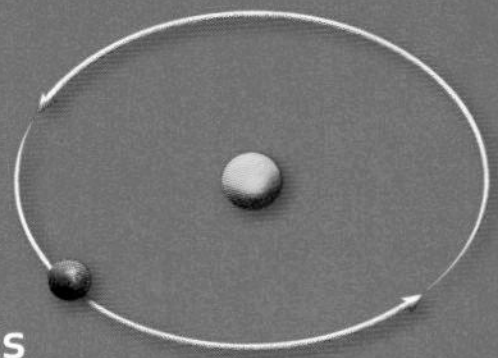

orbit
(ŌR-bit)

An **orbit** is the path Earth or another object takes in space as it revolves.

rotate
(RŌ-tāt)

To **rotate** is to spin around.

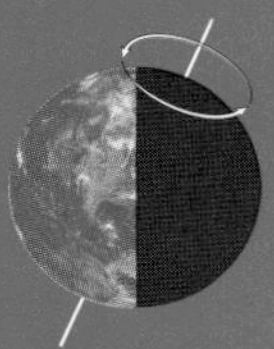

ROTATE

READY SET STAAR

READINESS STANDARD TEKS 5.8.C:
Demonstrate that Earth rotates on its axis once approximately every 24 hours causing the day/night cycle and the apparent movement of the Sun across the sky.

Earth **rotates** on its **axis.** A day on Earth is 24 hours—the length of time it takes Earth to complete one rotation.

DAY AND NIGHT

Earth never stops rotating. Earth makes one complete rotation approximately every 24 hours. It is daytime on the half of Earth that is facing the Sun. It is nighttime on the half of Earth that is facing away from the Sun.

APPARENT MOVEMENT

Every day and night, the Sun, Moon, and many stars appear to move across the sky. But it is really Earth that is rotating.

SHARE AND COMPARE

- Choose *revolve* or *rotate.* Have each person in your group draw a picture of Earth revolving or rotating.

- Next to your picture, describe a natural pattern that you can observe that is caused by that movement.

- Share your picture with others who chose a different movement or pattern. Describe any differences.

axis
(AK-sis)

An **axis** is an imaginary line around which Earth spins.

143

ENERGY RESEARCHER

Rebecca Dodder

How will energy be produced in the future? Rebecca Dodder is an energy researcher with the U.S. Environmental Protection Agency (EPA). She uses computer software to model what the future may look like. Her research helps others make good choices about energy.

NG Science: What is your job like?

Rebecca Dodder: I work with a team of scientists. My role is to study how we might use biofuels instead of fossil fuels. I look at ways we can use things like corn, trees, grasses, and algae as energy resources. For example, could we really use plants to make fuels to replace gasoline in our vehicles?

NG Science: What do you hope to accomplish?

Rebecca Dodder: I've always wanted to make life better for people. One way to do that is to protect the environment in which we live, breathe, work, and play.

Dodder researches questions such as "How does growing corn for biofuel affect the environment?"

This person is refueling her vehicle with ethanol, a type of biofuel made from corn. Ethanol is combined with regular gasoline.

biofuel

The Eastern Newt, or Red-spotted Newt, is a salamander that can be found throughout eastern North America. The immature newt goes through a stage known as the "red eft," in which its body is bright orange or red. Red efts can be found on land in moist forests. Adult newts can be found in lakes, marshes, and shallow ponds.

ORGANISMS AND ENVIRONMENTS

REPORTING CATEGORY 4: ORGANISMS AND ENVIRONMENTS

The student will demonstrate an understanding of the structures and functions of living organisms and their interdependence on each other and on their environment.

5.9 ORGANISMS and ENVIRONMENTS
The student knows that there are relationships, systems, and cycles within environments.

5.10 ORGANISMS and ENVIRONMENTS
The student knows that organisms undergo similar life processes and have structures that help them survive within their environments.

Coastal ECOSYSTEMS

This Texas beach is home to different kinds of animals and plants. All of the organisms on this beach interact with each other and the non-living elements in their environment. The non-living elements include sunlight, air, water, and sand. The living and non-living elements in the coastal environment form an ecosystem. Each of the organisms finds what it needs to live and survive in its coastal ecosystem.

ghost crab

Ghost crabs eat clams, young turtles, and even other crabs!

Kemp's ridley turtle

voCAB

ecosystem
(Ē-kō-sis-tum)

An ecosystem is all the living and non-living elements in an area.

This young turtle, or hatchling, is crawling to the ocean. It may return later in life to lay its eggs on this same beach.

READY SET STAAR

READINESS STANDARD TEKS 5.9.A:
Observe the way organisms live and survive in their ecosystem by interacting with the living and non-living elements.

How do the organisms in this photograph interact with their environment? The ghost crab finds insects and other crabs to eat. The turtle swims in the water. It may lay its eggs and bury them in the sand. The egret finds snakes, insects, and fish to eat. Each of these animals breathes air. The plants take in carbon dioxide from the air and water and nutrients from the soil.

This egret gets food, water, air, and space to live in its ecosystem.

egret

My science notebook **WRAP IT UP!**

1. **Define** What is an ecosystem?

2. **Recall** What are three non-living elements in this coastal ecosystem?

3. **Apply** How do organisms interact with the living and non-living elements in their ecosystem?

149

MARSH POPULATIONS and COMMUNITIES

If you visited the marsh in this photo, you might see a bird called an avocet. Chances are, others like it are nearby. Each avocet is part of a **population**. A population is all the individuals of a species that live in an area. Populations of many different species live here.

INDIVIDUAL
One organism, such as this avocet, is the smallest unit of an ecosystem.

POPULATION
All the avocets that live in one place are a population.

READY SET STAAR

SUPPORTING STANDARD TEKS 3.9.A:
Observe and describe the physical characteristics of environments and how they support populations and communities within an ecosystem.

The populations that live and interact in an area make up a **community.** The populations and communities in the marsh ecosystem are supported by the physical characteristics of the environment. The avocets breathe air. The plants take in water and nutrients from the soil. Each population and community in an ecosystem interacts with the living and non-living elements in the ecosystem to get what it needs to survive.

COMMUNITY
All the populations of organisms that live and interact in an area form a community.

ECOSYSTEM
All the living and non-living elements in the ecosystem interact with each other.

My science notebook

WRAP IT UP !

1. **Explain** Which is more complex, a population or a community? Explain.

2. **Predict** What might happen if a population of plants or animals is removed from a community?

3. **Explain** How do the physical characteristics of an environment help support the organisms that live there?

151

DESERT FOOD CHAIN

Each organism plays an important part in its environment. Every organism needs energy to survive. Some organisms get energy directly from the Sun. Some get energy from eating other organisms. A **food chain** is the path through which energy flows from one living thing to another. In the food chain shown here, use your finger to trace the path of energy through a desert ecosystem.

sunlight

ENERGY SOURCE
Sunlight is the source of energy for the food chain.

sagebrush

PRODUCER
Producers use energy from sunlight to make their food.

lubber grasshopper

CONSUMER
Some consumers get energ by eating sagebrush.

VoCAB

food chain
(fūd chān)

A **food chain** is the path through which energy flows from one organism to another in an ecosystem.

producer
(pruh-DŪS-ur)

A **producer** is an organism that makes its own food.

consumer
(kuhn-SŪ-mur)

A **consumer** is an organism that eats plants, animals, or both.

READY SET STAAR

READINESS STANDARD TEKS 5.9.B:
Describe how the flow of energy derived from the Sun, used by producers to create their own food, is transferred through a food chain and food web to consumers and decomposers.

The animal shown in this picture has died. When any organism in the food chain dies, **decomposers** such as bacteria and fungi cause the organism to decay. Decomposers can get energy from any part of the food chain. The decomposers use the energy they get from the dead organisms and release materials into the soil, air, or water. Nutrients released by decomposers can help new plants grow.

Texas horned lizard

CONSUMER
The Texas horned lizard gets energy by eating the grasshopper.

red-tailed hawk

CONSUMER
The hawk eats the lizard. The Sun's energy has moved through this food chain.

decomposer
(dē-kuhm-PŌZ-ur)

A **decomposer** is an organism that breaks down dead organisms and the waste of living things.

My science notebook WRAP IT UP!

1. **Recall** How is energy from the Sun transferred through a food chain?

2. **Describe** How do decomposers get energy?

3. **Explain** How are decomposers helpful to plants? How are plants helpful to decomposers?

DESERT FOOD WEB

A rattlesnake in this desert ecosystem eats animals such as mice and grasshoppers. These animals are part of the desert **food web**. A food web is a combination of food chains that shows how energy moves from the Sun through an ecosystem. Food webs show that organisms get energy from a variety of organisms.

Producers use energy from the Sun to make food. The energy is then passed on to different consumers and decomposers.

badger

cougar

grasshopper

voCAB

food web
(fūd web)

A food web is a combination of food chains that shows how energy moves from the Sun through an ecosystem.

154

READINESS STANDARD TEKS 5.9.B:
Describe how the flow of energy derived from the Sun, used by producers to create their own food, is transferred through a food chain and food web to consumers and decomposers.

READY SET STAAR

hawk

bighorn sheep

plants

rattlesnake

Trace the Energy!

The arrows show the direction in which energy moves through the food web. For example, plants get energy from sunlight. The bighorn sheep gets energy from plants. The cougar gets energy from the bighorn sheep. Use your finger to trace the energy through different food chains in the desert food web.

mouse

My science notebook

WRAP IT UP!

1. **Explain** How does energy flow through a food web?

2. **Contrast** How is a food web different from a food chain?

3. **Infer** Suppose a disease killed most of the red-tailed hawks in a desert area. What effect might that have on the area's animal life?

plants

155

INVESTIGATE
Interactions in a Model Pond

? How do living things in a model pond ecosystem interact?

An ecosystem is all the living and non-living elements in an area. You can create a model pond ecosystem in an aquarium or a terrarium. In this investigation, you can explore some of the interactions that take place in a model pond ecosystem.

MATERIALS

clear plastic bottle

sand

small rocks

Elodea

water

spoon

3 snails

hand lens

READY SET STAAR★

READINESS STANDARD TEKS 5.9.A:
Observe the way organisms live and survive in their ecosystem by interacting with the living and non-living elements.

READINESS STANDARD TEKS 5.9.B:
Describe how the flow of energy derived from the Sun, used by producers to create their own food, is transferred through a food chain and food web to consumers and decomposers.

1

Put sand and rocks at the bottom of a clear plastic bottle. Plant the *Elodea*. Pour water into the bottle until it is about two-thirds full. Use a spoon to place 3 snails in the model ecosystem.

2

my science notebook

Put your model in a sunny place. Observe the model each day for 7 days. Record your observations in your science notebook. Use a hand lens to observe changes in the ecosystem.

3

Use your observations to infer what each living thing needs and how it meets those needs. Classify each organism as a producer or consumer.

4

Draw your model pond ecosystem. Label the organisms. Draw arrows to show how energy moves from the Sun to the producers to the consumers in the model.

my science notebook

WRAP IT UP!

1. **Classify** How did your observations help you classify producers and consumers in your ecosystem?

2. **Explain** How did this model help you understand how organisms in a real pond ecosystem interact?

PLANTS INVADE!

The saltcedar plant grows in Europe, Asia, and Africa. People brought the plants to the United States to add beauty to the land. But saltcedar crowds out native trees and shrubs. Saltcedar is an **invasive organism** in Texas. An invasive organism is a living thing that does not belong in a certain place. Saltcedar harms the Texas environment.

saltcedar

Saltcedar absorbs large amounts of water. It makes deposits of salt that can harm the soil and other plants.

voCAB

invasive organism
(in-VĀ-siv OR-guh-niz-uhm)

An **invasive organism** is a living thing that does not belong in a place and can harm the environment.

SUPPORTING STANDARD TEKS 5.9.C: Predict the effects of changes in ecosystems caused by living organisms, including humans, such as the overpopulation of grazers or the building of highways.

Giant salvinia is a water plant that grows in South America. It was brought to the United States for use in aquariums and garden ponds. Giant salvinia grows quickly in Texas. It covers ponds, lakes, and rivers. Giant salvinia blocks sunlight that other native Texas plants need. It can reduce the amount of oxygen in the water. Organisms need oxygen to survive. Sometimes these organisms cannot survive in water covered with giant salvinia.

giant salvinia

My science *My* notebook

WRAP IT UP !

1. **Define** What is an invasive organism?

2. **Infer** How might fishing, boating, and swimming be affected by the growth of giant salvinia?

3. **Predict** What could happen if you bring a plant or animal from another place home to Texas?

159

ANIMALS INVADE!

Invasive plants can harm the environment. Invasive animals also cause harm. For example, people brought nutria from South America to Texas and other states to raise them for their furs. But many nutria escaped. They now live in Texas wetlands and eat plants that grow there. When nutria eat too many plants, no roots are left to hold soil in place. Then the soil can wash away.

nutria

Nutria can destroy wetlands by eating wetland plants. Then other animals that live in the wetlands do not have enough food to eat.

SUPPORTING STANDARD TEKS 5.9.C:
Predict the effects of changes in ecosystems caused by living organisms, including humans, such as the overpopulation of grazers or the building of highways.

The red imported fire ant is another invasive animal causing problems in Texas. These ants have a painful sting. They can kill young birds, mammals, and reptiles. They damage crops and can harm or kill young farm animals.

red imported
fire ant

RED IMPORTED FIRE ANTS IN TEXAS

2007

1985

1967

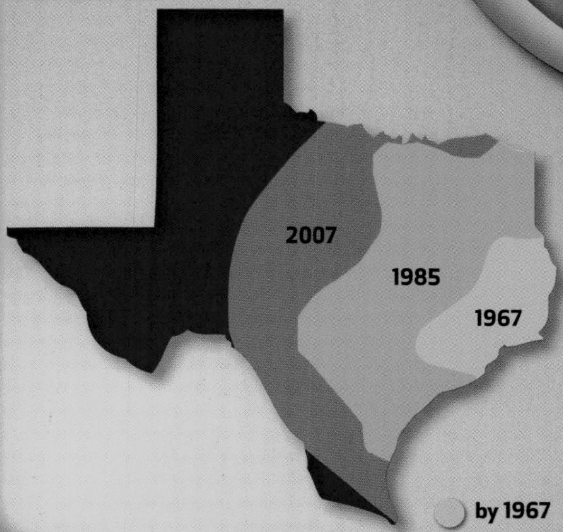

Red imported fire ants were first found in Texas in 1952. Look at the chart to the left. Describe how the ants have spread throughout the state.

by 1967   by 1985   by 2007

my science notebook

WRAP IT UP!

1. **Recall** What are some problems caused by red imported fire ants in Texas?

2. **Predict** What might happen to the fish, birds, and other living things in a wetland ecosystem when nutria are introduced?

PHORID FLIES MOVE IN!

phorid fly

In Texas, red imported fire ants do not have natural
enemies. In South America, phorid flies are an enemy of
red fire ants. Scientists have released phorid flies in Texas and other
southern states. When phorid flies come near fire ants, the ants try to
hide. The flies keep the ants from searching for food. With less food, the
fire ant population cannot grow. But why do fire ants hide from phorid flies?
It seems that around phorid flies, the fire ants just can't keep their heads on!

red imported
fire ant

SUPPORTING STANDARD TEKS 5.9.C:
Predict the effects of changes in ecosystems caused by living organisms, including humans, such as the overpopulation of grazers or the building of highways.

OFF WITH THEIR
HEADS!

1 A phorid fly lays an egg in the body of an ant. The egg hatches and the larva moves to the ant's head. It begins to eat the brain and other tissues. Like a zombie, the ant wanders away from the nest.

2 The larva releases an enzyme that causes the ant's head to fall off. The larva continues to feed and develops into a pupa.

3 Finally, as an adult, the phorid fly emerges from the ant's head.

My science notebook WRAP IT UP!

1. **Summarize** Describe how the phorid fly develops from an egg to an adult.

2. **Explain** How do phorid flies affect the behavior of red imported fire ants? How does this affect the red imported fire ant population?

MAKE WAY FOR HUMANS

Over the years, people have changed many ecosystems. One way that they have changed ecosystems is by clearing land for building highways. Many plants and animals lose their homes when people build highways. Then the plants and animals no longer have the food, water, or space they need to survive. The building of highways also uses large amounts of energy and resources, such as iron to make steel and rocks to make concrete. Today many people try to preserve habitats so that more plants and animals can survive.

Early Texas settlers may have seen ecosystems such as these wetlands shown in the photo. These ecosystems were changed when people built highways.

SUPPORTING STANDARD TEKS 5.9.C:
Predict the effects of changes in ecosystems caused by living organisms, including humans, such as the overpopulation of grazers or the building of highways.

There's the Beef!

About 14 million cattle are raised in Texas for their meat. That is more beef cattle than in any other state!

Another way that humans have changed Texas ecosystems is by raising grazing animals such as cattle. When many cattle graze for too long, the plants the cattle eat cannot grow back quickly enough. The soil cannot hold as much moisture as before. The soil can be blown or washed away. Invasive plants may begin to grow on overgrazed land. Responsible ranchers are careful not to let their cattle overgraze.

My science notebook WRAP IT UP!

1. **Predict** How can building highways affect Texas ecosystems?

2. **Predict** How can overgrazing affect the living and non-living things in a Texas grassland ecosystem?

INVESTIGATE PLANTS AND WATER

? How can a plant affect the water in its environment?

Plants can affect the environment in which they live and grow. Plants give off oxygen that we need to breathe. They can keep soil from being blown away by wind or washed away by water. Plants take up water through their roots and release water through their leaves. In this investigation, you can observe how a plant can affect the water in its environment.

MATERIALS

hand lens

plant cutting

index card with waxed paper

pencil

clay

plastic cup with water

plastic cup

black marker

SUPPORTING STANDARD TEKS 5.9.C:
Predict the effects of changes in ecosystems caused by living organisms, including humans, such as the overpopulation of grazers or the building of highways.

1 Use a hand lens to observe the plant cutting. Record your observations in your science notebook.

2 Use the pencil to make a small hole in the center of an index card and waxed paper. Hold the index card so that the waxed paper is on the bottom. Pull the stem of a plant cutting through the hole. Seal around the opening with clay.

3 Place the plant cutting in a cup of water. Make sure that the stem of the plant is in the water. Cover the top of the plant with another plastic cup. Mark the water level by drawing a line on the bottom cup.

4 Place the plant in a sunny spot. Observe the plant and cups after 24 and 48 hours. Record your observations. Compare your observations from different days.

WRAP IT UP!

1. **Describe** What happened in the cups after 24 hours and 48 hours?

2. **Conclude** What happens to some of the water that plants take in?

3. **Infer** How might plants affect the amount of groundwater? How might plants affect the amount of water in the air?

167

CARBON DIOXIDE-OXYGEN CYCLE

Look at the grasses and flowers in this meadow. Animals such as rabbits, mice, and deer may live here. All of the organisms in the meadow depend on each other for survival. The plants and animals of the meadow each play their part in the **carbon dioxide–oxygen cycle.** The carbon dioxide-oxygen cycle provides living things with the carbon dioxide and oxygen they need to survive.

oxygen

The plants give off oxygen that is needed by the white-tailed deer and other organisms.

plants

SUPPORTING STANDARD TEKS 5.9.D: Identify the significance of the carbon dioxide-oxygen cycle to the survival of plants and animals.

carbon dioxide

The white-tailed deer gives off carbon dioxide that can be used by plants.

white-tailed deer

My science notebook **WRAP IT UP!**

1. **Recall** What do animals give off that can be used by plants?

2. **Explain** Why is the carbon dioxide-oxygen cycle important to plants and animals?

169

HOOVES
ON THE PRAIRIE

One type of animal that lives on the prairie is the American bison. An American bison has certain body parts that help it live and survive. For example, its hooves are very hard. The hooves allow the American bison to walk over rocks and grasses. The hooves also provide support for the bison's long migration when it looks for food.

American bison

A bison has large hooves that support its great weight and help it walk across the prairie.

pronghorn

A pronghorn has small, hard hooves that help it run quickly and dodge predators on the prairie.

My science notebook

WRAP IT UP!

1. **Explain** How do hooves help the American bison and the pronghorn live and survive on the prairie?

2. **Compare** How are the American bison hooves and pronghorn hooves alike?

WEBBED FEET

A water ecosystem can support many different types of animals. One specialized body part that helps these animals survive is their webbed feet. In animals with webbed feet, there is a small piece of skin that stretches between each toe. Webbed feet allow animals to swim faster through the water to either catch food to eat or escape from predators.

Rio Grande leopard frog

The American alligator's webbed feet help it to make fast turns and sudden moves as it searches for prey.

American alligator

The webbed feet of the Rio Grande leopard frog allow it to swim easily through its ecosystem.

READY SET STAAR

READINESS STANDARD TEKS 5.10.A:
Compare the structures and functions of different species that help them live and survive such as hooves on prairie animals or webbed feet in aquatic animals.

Animals with webbed feet include amphibians such as frogs, and birds such as ducks, swans, and seagulls. Even some reptiles, such as turtles and alligators, have webbed feet, too!

red-eared slider turtle

The webbed feet of the red-eared slider turtle help it swim in the water. The only time it comes onto land is to lay eggs.

mallard duck

The mallard duck's webbed feet help it paddle through the water.

My science *notebook* **WRAP IT UP!**

1. **Explain** How do the frog's webbed feet help it survive in its ecosystem?

2. **Compare** How do the turtle and the duck use their webbed feet?

3. **Compare** How do hooves and webbed feet help organisms survive in their ecosystems?

173

PAWS AND CLAWS

Many different kinds of animals live in an ecosystem. Each of these animals has certain body parts that help it get what it needs. Read how paws and claws can help the animals in the pictures live and survive in their ecosystem.

A coyote has paws with pads that allow it to hunt quietly and not scare away its prey.

coyote

174

READINESS STANDARD TEKS 5.10.A:
Compare the structures and functions of
different species that help them live and
survive such as hooves on prairie animals
or webbed feet in aquatic animals.

CLAWS FOR GRASPING

A Harris's hawk holds its prey
with its long, sharp claws.
The claws are called talons.

Harris's hawk

CLAWS FOR DIGGING

A nine-banded armadillo uses
its claws for digging in the soil
to find insects to eat.

nine-banded armadillo

PAWS FOR HOPPING

A hare has long legs
and thin paws that help
it quickly hop away
from predators.

hare

My science notebook WRAP IT UP !

1. **Recall** How does the Harris's hawk use its talons
to survive?

2. **Compare** How are the paws of the coyote and the
claws of the nine-banded armadillo used differently?

175

INHERITED TRAITS

Most characteristics of organisms, such as eye color, body shape, and number of legs, are **inherited** traits. Inherited traits are characteristics that are passed down from parent to offspring. The shape of a bird's beak is an inherited trait. The shape of a young bird's beak is the same as the shape of its parent's beak. The size and shape of the bird's beak help the bird catch and eat its food.

bald eagle

hawfinch

whooping crane

The bald eagle inherits a hooked beak that helps the bird tear meat from its prey.

A seed-eater, such as the hawfinch, inherits a thick, cone-shaped beak that works like a nutcracker.

Whooping cranes use their long, sharp beaks to catch fish and insects. They also eat berries.

voCAB

inherited
(in-HAIR-it-ed)

An **inherited** trait is a characteristic that is passed down from parent to offspring.

READINESS STANDARD TEKS 5.10.B:
Differentiate between inherited traits of plants and animals such as spines on a cactus or shape of a beak and learned behaviors such as an animal learning tricks or a child riding a bicycle.

prickly pear cactus

The spines on a prickly pear cactus are an inherited trait. The spines help protect the plant from being eaten by animals.

young whooping crane

adult whooping crane

My science notebook

WRAP IT UP !

1. **Define** What is an inherited trait?

2. **Explain** How does the shape of the whooping crane's beak help it survive in its ecosystem?

3. **Explain** How do the spines of the prickly pear cactus help it survive in its ecosystem?

177

LEARNED BEHAVIORS

Many dogs are trained to help people. For example, they guide people who cannot see. These actions are **learned behaviors**. Learned behaviors are actions that come about through repeated experience.

Guide dogs are trained in very specific learned behaviors that help them lead and protect their owners who cannot see. For example, a guide dog may learn how to help its owner walk across the street, use an escalator, or enter a bus or subway.

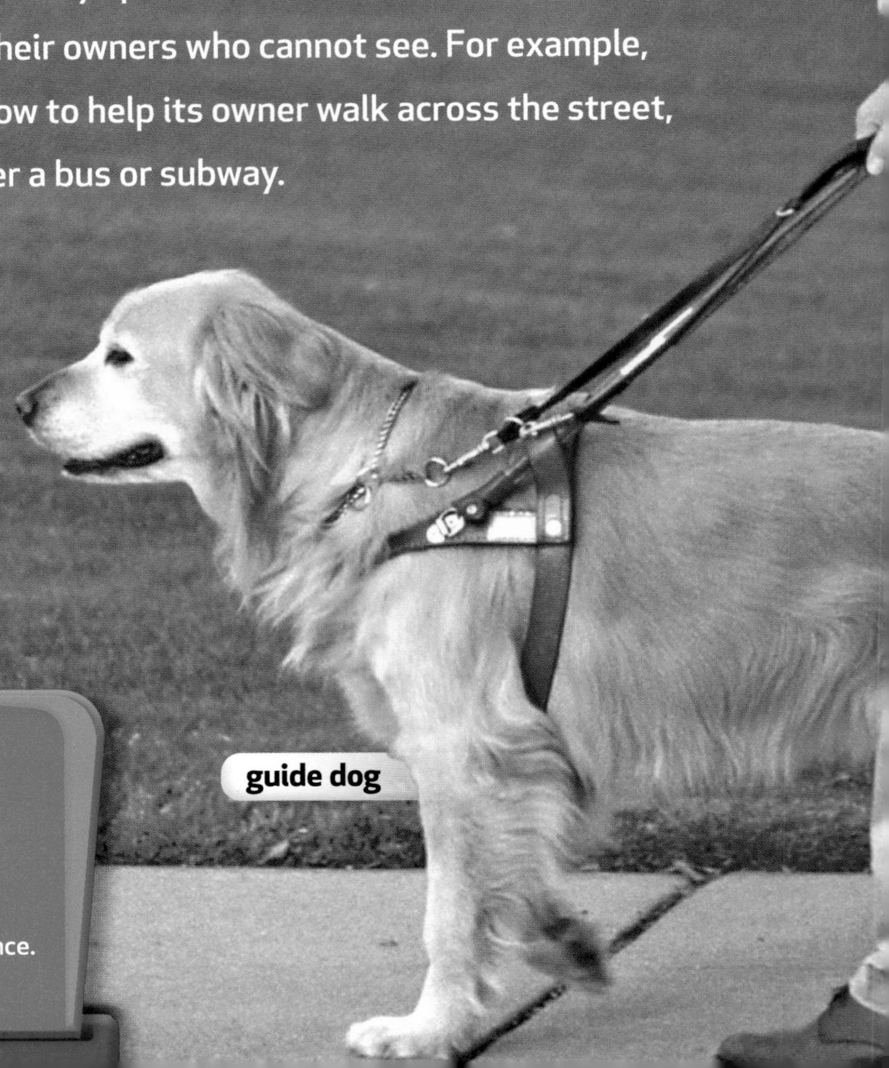

This guide dog helps its owner walk down the sidewalk.

guide dog

READINESS STANDARD TEKS 5.10.B:
Differentiate between inherited traits of plants and animals such as spines on a cactus or shape of a beak and learned behaviors such as an animal learning tricks or a child riding a bicycle.

Riding a bicycle is a learned behavior. People may remember this learned behavior for a long time.

This man has a GPS device in his backpack. The GPS device helps the man know his location.

My science notebook **WRAP IT UP !**

1. **Recall**   What is a learned behavior?

2. **Contrast**   What is the difference between an inherited trait and a learned behavior?

3. **Explain**   How does the special training guide dogs receive allow them to help their owners?

179

Life Cycle of an Eggplant

The eggplant is a flowering plant. The eggplant goes through many stages. These stages are called its life cycle. Review the life stages of a tomato plant. Then follow the diagram of the eggplant life cycle as you read.

Life Stages of a Tomato Plant

Seed

Seedling

Young Plant

Adult Plant

SUPPORTING STANDARD TEKS 3.10.C:
Investigate and compare how animals and
plants undergo a series of orderly changes
in their diverse life cycles such as tomato
plants, frogs, and ladybugs.

Seed

Like a tomato, the seeds
of an eggplant are found
in its fruit.

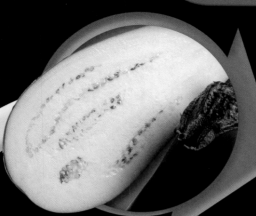

Adult Plant

Adult eggplants can
flower and produce
fruit called eggplants.

Life Cycle of an
Eggplant

Seedling

Eggplant seeds can
grow into seedlings
in warm, moist soil.

Young Plant

The seedling can grow
into a young plant with
many leaves.

My science notebook

WRAP IT UP!

1. **Define** What is a life cycle?

2. **Compare** How are the life stages of an eggplant
and a tomato plant alike? How are they different?

181

INVESTIGATE
The Life Cycle
of a Radish Plant

? **What are the stages in the life cycle of a radish?**

Living things undergo many changes during their lifetime. The stages in an organism's life are called its life cycle. In this investigation, you will observe the changes that occur during the life cycle of a radish plant.

MATERIALS

spoon   3 radish seeds   cup with soil   spray bottle with water   hand lens   brush

READY SET STAAR

SUPPORTING STANDARD TEKS 3.10.C:
Investigate and compare how animals and plants undergo a series of orderly changes in their diverse life cycles such as tomato plants, frogs, and ladybugs.

1

Use a spoon to plant 3 radish seeds in a cup with soil. Make sure that soil covers each seed. Keep the soil moist. Place the cup in a sunny place. Observe the cup each day. Record your observations in your science notebook.

My science notebook

2

When the seeds sprout, record your observations. Observe and draw the plant parts in your science notebook, noting how they change over time. Record your observations.

3

Use a hand lens to observe the parts of any flowers that form. Use a brush to move pollen from one flower to another. Moving pollen from flower to flower will allow seeds to form.

4

Continue to observe the flowers until seeds form. Use the hand lens to observe the seeds. Draw the life cycle of a radish plant based on your observations.

My science notebook

WRAP IT UP !

1. **Explain** What changes did you observe in the plants as they grew?

2. **Compare** How are the life cycles of the radish and tomato plant alike?

LIFE CYCLE OF A SALAMANDER

The spotted salamander is a large, dark gray amphibian with yellow or orange spots. It can grow up to 23 cm (9 in.) in length and live as long as 20 years! The spotted salamander lives in forests. Review the life stages of a frog. Then follow the diagram of the spotted salamander life cycle as you read.

LIFE STAGES OF A FROG

Egg   **Tadpole**   **Young Adult**   **Adult**

SUPPORTING STANDARD TEKS 3.10.C:
Investigate and compare how animals and
plants undergo a series of orderly changes
in their diverse life cycles such as tomato
plants, frogs, and ladybugs.

Egg
A female spotted
salamander lays
many eggs in a pond
or swamp.

Adult
Like a frog, an adult
spotted salamander
lives on land and uses
lungs to breathe air.

Life Cycle of a
SALAMANDER

Larva
A spotted
salamander larva
has a tail and no
legs. It breathes
under water
through gills.

Young Adult
The young spotted
salamander begins to
grow legs. During this
stage, the salamander
lives under water.

My science notebook **WRAP IT UP!**

1. **Contrast** Describe some differences between the
larva and adult stages of the spotted salamander.

2. **Compare** How are the life stages of the spotted
salamander similar to the life stages of a frog?

185

COMPLETE
Metamorphosis

Some kinds of animals go through **metamorphosis** as they grow.
Metamorphosis is a series of changes in an animal's body over time.
The bodies of some insects go through four stages as they develop.
They go through complete metamorphosis. Find the
picture of the egg stage of the monarch butterfly.
Trace the butterfly's life stages with your finger.

The Life of a Monarch Butterfly

Egg · · · · · · · ·
A female butterfly
lays eggs on or near
a milkweed plant.

Larva · · · · · · · · · ·
The **larva** hatches from
an egg. The larva looks
different from the adult.
The larva eats milkweed
leaves and grows quickly.

vOCAB

metamorphosis
(met-ah-MOR-fah-sis)

Metamorphosis is
a series of changes in an
animal's body form during
its life cycle.

larva
(LAR-va)

A **larva** is a young
animal with a body form
different from the adult.

pupa
(PŪ-pah)

A **pupa** is the
stage in which
the body of a young
animal changes from
the larva to the adult.

monarch butterfly

Pupa

In the **pupa** stage, the insect changes from a larva into an adult. The pupa does not eat.

Adult

The pupa becomes an adult monarch butterfly. The adult feeds on nectar from flowers.

My science notebook

WRAP IT UP!

1. **Recall** What are the life stages of an insect that goes through complete metamorphosis?

2. **Contrast** Describe some differences between the larva and the adult monarch butterfly.

3. **Infer** An adult female monarch butterfly lays eggs on a milkweed plant. How do you think this benefits the larva?

INCOMPLETE
Metamorphosis

Some animals go through incomplete metamorphosis. Their bodies only go through three stages as they develop. The three stages are egg, **nymph,** and adult. The nymph and the adult look almost the same. But the nymph may not have all the features an adult has. For example, a praying mantis adult has wings. The nymph does not.

The Life of a Praying Mantis

Egg . . . . . ▶ Nymph . . . .

The female lays many eggs. The eggs are in a case that protects them.

The nymph looks like the adult. As the nymph grows, its hard outer covering becomes too small. It begins to grow a new covering. It molts, or sheds the old covering. A nymph may molt many times before it finally emerges as an adult.

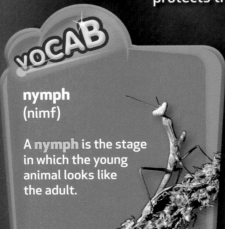

VOCAB

nymph
(nimf)

A **nymph** is the stage in which the young animal looks like the adult.

SUPPORTING STANDARD TEKS 5.10.C:
Describe the differences between complete
and incomplete metamorphosis of insects.

Here's Looking at You!

The praying mantis can turn its head. It can look in different directions without moving the rest of its body.

►Adult

Insects that go through incomplete metamorphosis do not have a pupa stage. After a final molting, the insect is an adult. The adult praying mantis has wings.

My science notebook

WRAP IT UP !

1. **Summarize** Describe each stage of incomplete metamorphosis.

2. **Contrast** How is complete metamorphosis different from incomplete metamorphosis?

189

COMPLETE METAMORPHOSIS
LADYBUG

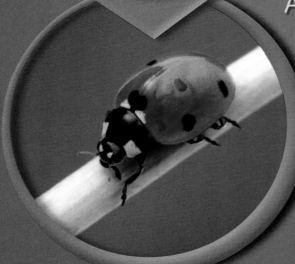

Egg The first stage in a ladybug's life is the egg. Each tiny egg is about twice as big as the head of a pin.

Larva The ladybug **larva** hatches from an egg. Its body has a narrow shape. It sheds its covering many times during this stage.

Pupa Then the larva grows a hard shell. The **pupa** stage begins. The ladybug pupa is about the same size as the adult. This stage lasts 5-7 days.

Adult Adult ladybugs have wings and can fly. Adult ladybugs look very different than they do during the larva stage. They eat many different types of insects.

voCAB

larva
(LAR-va)

A **larva** is a young animal with a body form different from the adult.

pupa
(PŪ-pah)

A **pupa** is the stage of a life cycle in which the body form of a young animal changes from the

INCOMPLETE
METAMORPHOSIS
DRAGONFLY

SUPPORTING STANDARD TEKS 5.10.C:
Describe the differences between complete
and incomplete metamorphosis of insects.

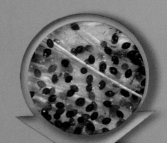

Egg The adult female dragonfly
lays eggs in water or on a
water plant.

Nymph The young dragonfly, or **nymph,**
hatches from an egg. The nymph
lives in water and breathes through
gills. It eats insect larvae and other
living things. As it grows, a new
covering forms. The nymph then
molts, or sheds, its old covering.

Adult The dragonfly has become an adult
with wings. It lives on land. The adult
looks very different than it did as
a nymph.

SHARE AND COMPARE

- Choose an insect. Have each person
  in your group draw a picture of
  a different stage in its life.

- Arrange the pictures to show the
  order of the stages.

- Share your pictures with another
  group. Does your insect go
  through complete or incomplete
  metamorphosis? Explain.

VOCAB

nymph
(nimf)

A **nymph** is the stage
in which the young
animal looks like
the adult.

191

LEPIDOPTERIST

Dr. Karen Oberhauser

Would you like to be a lepidopterist? A lepidopterist is a person who studies butterflies! Dr. Karen Oberhauser is a lepidopterist. She studies monarch butterflies and teaches college classes about them. She also teaches people how to protect monarch butterflies.

NG Science: What do you like most about your job?

Dr. Oberhauser: I've studied many features of monarch butterflies, from how they reproduce to how they migrate. It's been fun to become an expert on this butterfly. I've also loved teaching people how important it is to preserve the natural world for the future.

NG Science: What has been your greatest accomplishment in your job?

Dr. Oberhauser: I have worked to get people to help collect data about monarch butterflies. My goal has been to conserve as much of the natural world as possible. I feel that one way I have done that is by helping people see the wonder of natural environments.

Flutter By, Butterfly!. . . .

Many monarch butterflies migrate through Texas on their way to Mexico. Some monarchs migrate almost 5,000 kilometers (about 3,000 miles)!

monarch butterfly

People all over the United States help Dr. Oberhauser collect data. Having lots of data helps scientists make good inferences and conclusions.

scales

Butterflies' wings are made of thousands of tiny scales. How would you describe these scales that have been magnified with a microscope?

GLOSSARY

A

alternative energy resource (awl-TUR-nuh-tiv EN-ur-jē RĒ-sors)

An alternative energy resource is a source of energy that can be used in place of fossil fuels. (p. 102)

apparent movement (uh-PAIR-ent MOOV-ment)

An object's apparent movement is the way it appears to move, not whether or how it actually moves. (p. 132)

axis (AK-sis)

An axis is an imaginary line around which Earth spins. (pp. 130, 143)

B

biofuel (BĪ-ō-fyū-ul)

A biofuel is any fuel made from plant material or animal waste. (p. 110)

C

canyon (KAN-yen)

A canyon is a deep, narrow valley with steep sides that is formed by flowing water. (p. 66)

carbon dioxide–oxygen cycle (KAR-bin dī-AHKS-īde AHKS-i-jin SĪ-kul)

The carbon dioxide–oxygen cycle provides organisms with the carbon dioxide and oxygen they need to survive. (p. 168)

climate (KLĪ-mit)

Climate is the pattern of weather of an area over a long period of time. (pp. 116, 119)

community (kuh-MYŪ-nuh-tē)

A community is made up of all the different populations that live and interact in an area. (p. 150)

conservation (kon-suhr-VĀ-shun)

Conservation is the protection and care of natural resources. (p. 88)

consumer (kuhn-SŪ-mur)

A consumer is an organism that eats plants, animals, or both. (p. 152)

D

decomposer (dē-kuhm-PŌZ-ur)

A decomposer is an organism that breaks down dead organisms and the waste of living things. (p. 153)

delta (DEL-tuh)

A delta is new land that forms at the mouth of a river. (p. 66)

density (DEN-si-tē)

Density is the measure of the amount of matter in a certain amount of space. (p. 10)

deposition (de-pō-ZI-shun)

Deposition is the laying down of rock and soil in a new place. (p. 70)

E

ecosystem (Ē-kō-sis-tum)

An ecosystem is all the living and non-living things in an area. (p. 148)

electrical circuit (i-LEK-tri-kul SUR-kuht)

An electrical circuit is a complete path through which electric current can pass. (p. 44)

electrical conductor (i-LEK-tri-kul kon-DUK-ter)

An electrical conductor is a material through which electrical energy can flow easily. (p. 16)

electrical energy (i-LEK-tri-kul EN-ur-jē)

Electrical energy is the energy of moving charged particles. (pp. 16, 42)

electrical insulator (i-LEK-tri-kul IN-su-lā-ter)

An electrical insulator is a material that slows or stops the flow of electricity. (p. 16)

erosion (ē-RŌ-zhun)

Erosion is the picking up and moving of rocks and soil to a new place. (p. 70)

F

experiment (ex-PAIR-i-ment)

An experiment is an investigation in which variables are manipulated and controlled. (p. 54)

food chain (fūd chān)

A food chain is the path through which energy flows from one organism to another in an ecosystem. (p. 152)

food web (fūd web)

A food web is a combination of food chains that shows how energy moves from the Sun through an ecosystem. (p. 154)

fossil fuel (FOS-ul FYŪ-ul)

A fossil fuel is a source of energy formed from the remains of plants and animals that lived millions of years ago. (p. 86)

G

geothermal energy (jē-ō-THER-mul EN-ur-jē)

Geothermal energy is heat energy from within Earth. (p. 108)

H

hydroelectric power (hī-drō-i-LEK-trik POW-ur)

Hydroelectric power is electricity produced by the energy in moving water. (p. 106)

hypothesis (hī-POTH-i-sis)

A hypothesis is a statement that gives a possible answer to a question that can be tested by an experiment. (p. 56)

I

inherited (in-HAIR-it-ed)

An inherited trait is a characteristic that is passed down from parent to offspring. (p. 176)

invasive organism (in-VĀ-siv OR-guh-niz-uhm)

An invasive organism is a living thing that does not belong in a place and can harm the environment. (p. 158)

L

landform (LAND-form)

A landform is a natural feature on Earth's surface. (p. 66)

larva (LAR-va)

A larva is a young animal with a body form different from the adult. (pp. 186, 190)

learned behaviors (LURND bē-HĀV-yurs)

Learned behaviors are actions that come about through repeated experience. (p. 178)

light energy (LĪT EN-ur-jē)

Light energy is energy that you can see. (p. 30)

M

magnetism (MAG-nuh-ti-zuhm)

Magnetism is a force produced by magnets that pulls some metals. (p. 6)

mass (MAS)

Mass is the amount of matter in an object. (p. 4)

matter (MA-tur)

Matter is anything that has mass and takes up space. (p. 4)

mechanical energy (mi-KAN-i-kul EN-ur-jē)

Mechanical energy includes energy an object has because of its motion. (p. 28)

metamorphosis (met-ah-MOR-fah-sis)

Metamorphosis is a series of changes in an animal's body form during its life cycle. (p. 186)

N

nonrenewable resources (non-rē-NŪ-uh-bul RĒ-sors-es)

Nonrenewable resources are those that cannot be replaced quickly enough to keep from running out. (p. 86)

nymph (nimf)

A nymph is the stage in which the young animal looks like the adult. (pp. 188, 191)

O

orbit (ŌR-bit)

An orbit is the path Earth or another object takes in space as it revolves. (pp. 126, 142)

P

population (pop-yū-LĀ-shun)

A population is all the individuals of a species that live in an area. (p. 150)

producer (pruh-DŪS-ur)

A producer is an organism that makes its own food. (p. 152)

pulley (PUL-lē)

A pulley is a grooved wheel with a cable or a rope running through the groove. (p. 48)

pupa (PŪ-pah)

A pupa is the stage in which the body of a young animal changes from the larva to the adult. (pp. 186, 190)

R

reflection (rē-FLEK-shun)

Reflection is the bouncing of light off an object. (p. 34)

refraction (rē-FRAK-shun)

Refraction is the bending of light when it moves through one medium to another. (p. 36)

renewable resources (rē-NŪ-uh-bul RĒ-sors-es)

Renewable resources are those that are always being replaced and will not run out. (p. 86)

revolve (re-VAWLV)

To revolve is to travel around another object in space. (pp. 126, 142)

rotate (RŌ-tāt)

To rotate is to spin around. (pp. 130, 142)

S

sand dune (SAND DŪN)

A sand dune is a hill of sand formed by wind. (p. 67)

sediment (SED-ah-mint)

Sediment is material that comes from the weathering of rock. (p. 70)

sedimentary rock (sed-i-MEN-tah-rē ROK)

Many sedimentary rocks form from small pieces of rocks and minerals that are cemented together. (p. 94)

sound energy (SOWND EN-ur-jē)

Sound energy is energy that you can hear. (p. 40)

T

thermal conductor (THUR-mul kon-DUK-ter)

A thermal conductor is a material that heats up quickly. (p. 14)

thermal energy (THUR-mul EN-ur-jē)

Thermal energy is the energy of vibrating, or moving, particles. (pp. 14, 38)

thermal insulator (THUR-mul IN-su-lā-ter)

A thermal insulator is a material that heats up slowly. (p. 14)

tsunami ([t]sū-NAH-mē)

A tsunami is a series of ocean waves caused by an underwater earthquake or landslide. (p. 82)

V

variable (VAIR-ē-u-bul)

A variable is something that can change in an experiment. (p. 54)

W

water cycle (WAH-tur SĪ-kul)

The water cycle is the movement of water from Earth's surface to the air and back again. (p. 124)

weather (WE-thur)

Weather is the state of the atmosphere at a certain place and time. (pp. 114, 118)

weathering (WE-thur-ing)

Weathering is the breaking apart, wearing away, or dissolving of rock. (p. 68)

work (WERK)

Work is done when a force is used to move an object over a distance. (p. 48)

INDEX

Photographs

Front Matter

Title Page ©Tim Fitzharris/Minden Pictures/National Geographic Stock. **ii** (br) ©Vince Streano/Getty Images. (tl) ©NASA Human Space Flight Gallery. **iii** (br) ©narivkk/iStockphoto. (cl) ©Tom Begasse/Shutterstock. (tl) ©Serdar Yagci/iStockphoto. **iv** (tl) ©Claus Lunau/Bonnier Publications/Photo Researchers, Inc. (bl) ©Steve Wignall/iStockphoto. (tr) ©Michael Haegele/Corbis. (br) ©Thomas Northcut/Getty Images. **v** (tl) ©George Diebold/Getty Images. (bl) ©Todd Gipstein/National Geographic Stock. (tr) ©James Steidl/Shutterstock. (br) ©Joel Sartore/National Geographic Stock. **vi** (br) ©Jon Vidar Sigurdsson/Nordic Photos/Getty Images. (cl) ©LeighSmithImages/Alamy. (cr) ©Creatas/Jupiterimages. (tl) ©Radius Images/Corbis. **vii** (br) ©Bob Daemmrich/Corbis. (cl) ©Royik Yevgen/Shutterstock. (tl) ©Vadim Ponomarenko/Shutterstock. (tr) ©Paul Andrew Lawrence/Alamy. **viii** (cl) ©Tom Till/Getty Images. (cr) ©Jim Parkin/Shutterstock. (tl) ©inga spence/Alamy. **ix** (br) ©Dave Reede/AgStock Images/Corbis. (cl) ©Suvrangshu Ghosh/Your Shot/National Geographic Stock. (tl) ©NASA. (tr) ©Nancy Camel/Alamy. **x** (tr) ©DLILLC/Corbis. (br) ©Patrick Lynch/Alamy. (tl) ©Huey, George H.H./Animals Animals/Earth Scenes. (bl) ©Neil Holmes/Gap Photo/Visuals Unlimited, Inc. **xi** (tl) ©Rolf Nussbaumer/Nature Picture Library. (bl) ©Medford Taylor/National Geographic Stock. (tr) ©Joseph Sohm/Visions of America/Corbis. (br) ©Paul Sutherland/National Geographic Stock.

Reporting Category 1: Matter and Energy

2 ©Patrick Bennett/Corbis. **4** (b) ©Jeffery Stone/Shutterstock. (bkg) ©NASA Human Space Flight Gallery. **5** (bl) ©Baloncici/Shutterstock. (cr) ©Jeffery Stone/Shutterstock. **8** (bkg) ©Sun Star/Getty Images. **12** (bkg) ©Evgeny Kuklev/iStockphoto. **14** (bkg) ©Vince Streano/Getty Images. (bl) ©Sarah Winterflood/iStockphoto. (br) ©Dave King/Dorling Kindersley/Getty Images. **15** (tcl) ©Sarah Winterflood/iStockphoto. (tcr) ©Dave King/Dorling Kindersley/Getty Images. (tl) ©Stefano Scata/FoodPix/Getty Images. (tr) ©Thomas Collins/Getty Images. **16** (bkg) ©gh19/Shutterstock. (br) ©ID1974/Shutterstock. (tl) ©Serdar Yagci/iStockphoto. **17** (cr) ©Serdar Yagci/iStockphoto. (tcl) ©Daniel Tang/iStockphoto. (tcr) ©Yury Kosourov/Shutterstock. (tr) ©ID1974/Shutterstock. **18** (bkg) ©Gerhard Zwerger-Schoner/imagebroker/Alamy. (c) ©Tom Begasse/Shutterstock. **19** (c) ©John Burcham/National Geographic Stock. **20** (bkg) ©Sebastian Duda/Shutterstock. **22** (bkg) ©mycola/Shutterstock. **24** (bkg) ©narivkk/iStockphoto. (tl) ©Carol M. Grosvenor, 2009/Department of Mechanical Engineering, The University of Texas at Austin. **25** (tl) ©Pasieka/Photo Researchers, Inc.

Reporting Category 2: Force, Motion, and Energy

26 ©Carolyn Brown/Getty Images. **28** (bkg) ©Medioimages/Photodisc/Getty Images. **29** (cr) ©Claus Lunau/Bonnier Publications/Photo Researchers, Inc. **30** (bkg) ©Thomas Frey/imagebroker/Alamy. **31** (c) ©Anatoly Vartanov/Shutterstock. (cl) ©Don Klumpp/Getty Images. (cr) ©Radius Images/Alamy. **32** (bkg) ©Mark Axcell/Alamy. **34** (bkg) ©Steve Wignall/iStockphoto. **36** (b) ©Glowimages/Getty Images. (bkg) ©Glowimages/Getty Images. **38** (bkg) ©David Spurdens/Corbis. **39** (cr) ©Michael Haegele/Corbis. (tc) ©luckypic/Shutterstock. **40** (b) ©Timothy Bethke/Alamy. (bkg) ©A. T. Willett/Alamy. (c) ©Timothy Bethke/Alamy. **41** (cl) ©Dan Callister/Alamy. (cr) ©Clynt Garnham Lifestyle/Alamy. **42** (bkg) ©Adam Jones/Getty Images. **43** (cl) ©Westend61 GmbH/Alamy Images. (cr) ©Thomas Northcut/Getty Images. **44** (bkg) ©George Diebold/Getty Images. **46** (bkg) ©David Sanger/Jupiterimages. **48** (b) ©Rick Rhay/iStockphoto. (bkg) ©FRANCK FIFE/AFP/Getty Images. **49** (cr) ©Rick Rhay/iStockphoto. **50** (bkg) ©Todd Gipstein/National Geographic Stock. **52** (bkg) ©James Steidl/Shutterstock. **53** (cl) ©Pete Titmuss/Alamy. (cr) ©Rick Gomez/Corbis. **54** ©Newmann/Corbis. **55** (br) ©WilleeCole/Shutterstock. (c) ©Jan Rihak/istockphoto. (cl) ©WilleeCole/Shutterstock. **56** (cl) ©WilleeCole/Shutterstock. **58** (bkg) ©Jan Rihak/istockphoto. **59** (bkg) ©Jan Rihak/istockphoto. **62** (bkg) ©Joel Sartore/National Geographic Stock. (tl) ©Wake Forest University/Ken Bennett/Dr. William Conner. **63** (tl) ©Nickolay Hristov/Nickolay Hristov PhD.

Reporting Category 3: Earth and Space

64 ©Tim Fitzharris/Minden Pictures/National Geographic Stock. **66** (bkg) ©Kazuyoshi Nomachi/Corbis. (bl) ©James Parker. (br) ©David Noble/nobleIMAGES/Alamy. **67** (bcl)©James Steinberg/Photo Researchers, Inc. (bl) ©Gerald & Buff Corsi/Visuals Unlimited. (bl) ©Kazuyoshi Nomachi/Corbis. (cl) ©James L. Stanfield/National Geographic Stock. (tcl) ©James Parker. (tl) ©David Noble/nobleIMAGES/Alamy. **68** (bl) ©Radius Images/Corbis. (bkg) ©Radius Images/Corbis. **69** (c) ©David Boyer/National Geographic Stock. **70** (b) ©James Randklev/Corbis. (bkg) ©James Randklev/Corbis. **72** (bkg) ©Carr Clifton/Minden Pictures/National Geographic Stock. (c) ©LeighSmithImages/Alamy. **74** (bkg) ©Ian Shive/Aurora/Getty Images. **75** (c) ©Eric Foltz/iStockphoto. **76** (bkg) ©Cameron Davidson/Getty Images. **77** (c) ©Planet Observer/Photolibrary. **78** (bkg) ©Creatas/Jupiterimages. **79** (c) ©Carr Clifton/Minden Pictures/National Geographic Stock. (cl) ©Shubroto Chattopadhyay/Corbis RF/Alamy. (cr) ©Alex Neauville/Shutterstock. **80** (bkg) ©Jon Vidar Sigurdsson/Nordic Photos/Getty Images. (bl) ©STR/Reuters/Corbis. (cr) ©Jon Snorrason/epa/Corbis. **82** (bkg) ©Koichi Kamoshida/ZUMA Press/Corbis. **83** (c) ©Mainichi Shimbun/Reuters. **84** (bkg) ©Adek Berry/AFP/Getty Images. (bl) ©Andrew Gransden/Alamy. **86** (bc) ©Vadim Ponomarenko/Shutterstock. (bkg) ©Peter Miller/Getty Images. (bl) ©David Sucsy/iStockphoto. (br) ©Neil Beer/Photodisc/Getty Images. (cl) ©David Sucsy/iStockphoto. (cr) ©Dex Image/Alamy. (l) ©Steve Cole/iStockphoto. (r)©David R. Frazier/Photo Researchers, Inc. **87** (cl) ©Vadim Ponomarenko/Shutterstock. (cr) ©Neil Beer/Photodisc/Getty Images. (l) ©Raymond Gehman/National Geographic Stock. **88** (bkg)©David R. Frazier Photolibrary, Inc./Alamy. **89** (br) ©Charles O. Cecil/Alamy. (c) ©Alex Lentati/Evening Standard/Rex Features/Daily Mail/Rex/Alamy. **92** (bkg) ©Royik Yevgen/Shutterstock. **94** (b) ©Marc Adamus/Aurora/Getty Images. (bkg) ©Marc Adamus/Aurora/Getty Images. **95** (cl) ©Inge Johnsson/Alamy. (cr) ©Mike Brake/Shutterstock. **96** (bkg) ©Scott Camazine/Alamy. **98** (bkg) ©Paul Andrew Lawrence/Alamy. **100** (bkg) ©Poulides/Thatcher/Getty Images. **102** ©Joel Satore/National Geographic Stock. **104** (cl) ©Bob Daemmrich/Corbis. **106** (bkg) ©Harald Sund/Getty Images. **108** (bkg) ©Philippe Michel/age footstock. **110** (bkg) ©Jorge Moro/Shutterstock. **111** (c) ©Car Culture/Corbis. (cr) ©inga spence/Alamy (ctl) ©Sarah Leen/National Geographic Stock. **112** (bkg) ©Sarah Leen/National Geographic Stock. **113** (bl) ©Piotr Tomicki/Shutterstock (cbl) ©Snorri Gunnarsson/Alamy. (cl) ©Bill Hatcher/National Geographic Stock. (tl) ©Sarah Leen/National Geographic Stock. **114** (bkg) ©Lance Varnell/National Geographic Stock. (cl) ©Tom Till/Getty Images. (cr) ©Tim Fitzharris/Minden Pictures/National Geographic Stock. **116** (bkg) ©Jim

Parkin/Shutterstock. **117** (cl) ©Chad Ehlers/Alamy. (cr) ©Francisco Romero/istockphoto. (l) ©William Manning/Alamy. (tl) ©Jim Parkin/Shutterstock. (tr) ©Bob Daemmrich/Corbis. **118** (b) ©David Sanger/Getty Images. (cl) ©nagelestock.com/Alamy. (cr) ©Brad Perks Lightscapes/Alamy. (t) ©David R. Frazier Photolibrary, Inc./Alamy. **119** (bkg) ©Buddy Mays/Alamy. (bl) ©Ei Katsumata - FLP/Alamy. (cr) ©Tim Laman/National Geographic Stock. (tl) ©Jason Gayman/iStockphoto. **120** (bkg) ©Design Pics Inc./Alamy. **122** (bkg) ©Neil Overy/Getty Images. **124** (bkg) ©Bill Heinsohn/Alamy. (br) ©Alexei Fateev/Alamy. (tr) ©Frank, R./Arco Images GmbH/Alamy. **125** (bl) ©Derek Croucher/Alamy. (c) ©Jim Reed/Digital Vision/Getty Images. **126** (bkg) ©NASA. **128** (bkg) ©rotofrank/istockphoto. (l) ©Artville. **129** (c) ©PhotoDisc/Getty Images. (cl) ©Creatas/Jupiterimages. (cr) ©DigitalStock/Corbis. **130** (bkg) ©Alexandr Tovstenko/iStockphoto. **132** (bkg) ©Suvrangshu Ghosh/Your Shot/National Geographic Stock. **134** (bkg) ©Ken Schulze/Shutterstock. **136** (bc) ©Gary Buss/Getty Images. (bkg) ©Gary Buss/Getty Images. (bl) ©Gary Buss/Getty Images. (br) ©Gary Buss/Getty Images. **137** ©Gary Buss/Getty Images. **138** (bkg) ©Nancy Camel/Alamy. **139** (cr) ©Brian Yarvin/Photo Researchers, Inc. **140** (bkg) DigitalStock/Corbis. **142** (bkg) ©maxrosoftig/Shutterstock. **143** (bkg) ©maxrosoftig/Shutterstock. **144** (bkg) ©Dave Reede/AgStock Images/Corbis. (tl) ©John Masters/U.S. Environmental Protection Agency. **145** (br) ©Jim West/Alamy.

Reporting Category 4: Organisms and Environments
146 ©David Wrobel/Visuals Unlimited/Corbis. **148** (bkg) ©Tony Campbell/Shutterstock. (c) ©Jesse Cancelmo/Alamy. (cl) ©Huey, George H.H./Animals Animals/Earth Scenes. **150** (bkg) ©Doug Wechsler/VIREO. (bl) ©Tim Laman/National Geographic Stock. (cl) ©R. & N. Bowers/VIREO. (cr) ©Tim Laman/National Geographic Stock. **151** (cl) ©Doug Wechsler/VIREO. (cr) ©Doug Wechsler/VIREO. **152** (bc) ©Brendan Bucy/Shutterstock. (bkg) ©Ed Darack/Science Faction/Getty Images. (br) ©Barry Mansell/Nature Picture Library. (c) ©Brendan Bucy/Shutterstock. (cl) ©BLOOMimage/Getty Images. (cr) ©Barry Mansell/Nature Picture Library. **153** (cl) ©Rusty Dodson/Shutterstock. (cr) ©James McLaughlin/Alamy Images. (tl) ©Buddy Mays/Corbis. **154** (bkg) ©Tim Fitzharris/Minden Pictures/National Geographic Stock. (br) ©Chris Howes/Wild Places Photography/Alamy. (cl) ©DLILLC/Corbis. (cr) ©Jeff Vanuga/Corbis. **155** (bl) ©Rich Reid/National Geographic Stock. (cl) ©Jack Goldfarb/Design Pics/Corbis. (tl) ©Geostock/Photodisc/Getty Images. (tr) ©Rich Reid/National Geographic Stock. **156** (bkg) ©Jill Stephenson / Alamy. **158** (bkg) ©Dennis Frates/Alamy. (bl) ©AP Photo/Texas Parks and Wildlife/Rhandy Helton. (cr) ©Neil Holmes/Gap Photo/Visuals Unlimited, Inc. **159** (c) ©AP Photo/Pat Sullivan. (cl) ©AP Photo/Texas Parks and Wildlife/Rhandy Helton. **160** (bkg) ©James H. Robinson/Photo Researchers, Inc. **161** (tr) ©Patrick Lynch/Alamy. **162** (bkg) ©John C. Abbott/John C. Abbott Nature Photography. **163** (bl) ©Sanford Porter/Agricultural Research Service, USDA. (cl) ©Sanford Porter/Agricultural Research Service, USDA. (tl) ©Precision Graphics. **164** (bkg) ©David R. Frazier Photolibrary, Inc./Alamy. (bl) ©Brian Miller/Time Life Pictures/Getty Images. **165** (cr) ©Joel Sartore/National Geographic Stock. (tl) ©Sam Wirzba/AgStock Images/Corbis. **166** (bkg) ©Creatas/Jupiterimages. **168** (bkg) ©Linda Freshwaters Arndt/Alamy. **170** (bkg) ©Mills Tandy/Oxford Scientific/Getty Images. (br) ©Pete Oxford/Minden Pictures/National Geographic Stock. (c) ©Pete Oxford/Minden Pictures/National Geographic Stock. **171** (cl) ©franzfoto.com/Alamy. (cr) ©franzfoto.

com/Alamy. **172** (bkg) ©Michael Durham/Minden Pictures. (bl) ©Kevin Schafer/Alamy. (br) ©Kevin Schafer/Alamy. **173** (bbl) ©Naturepix/Alamy. (bl) ©Naturepix/Alamy. (cl) ©James Sparshatt/Axiom Photographic Agency/Getty Images. (cr) ©James Sparshatt/Axiom Photographic Agency/Getty Images. **174** (bkg) ©Brand X Pictures/photolibrary.com. **175** (bc) ©John Short/Design Pics/photolibrary.com. (cr) ©Rolf Nussbaumer/Nature Picture Library. (tc) ©Fred J. Lord/Jaynes Gallery/Danita Delimont/Alamy. **176** (bkg) ©Klaus Nigge/National Geographic Stock. (bl) ©Klaus Nigge/National Geographic Stock. (c) ©Maksym Gorpenyuk/Shutterstock. (cl) ©Creatas/Jupiterimages. (cr) ©Klaus Nigge/National Geographic Stock. **177** (tr) ©Joseph Sohm; ChromoSohm Inc./Corbis. **178** (bkg) ©Mark Richards/PhotoEdit. **179** (tr) ©Polka Dot Images/Jupiterimages. **180** (bcl) ©Liza McCorkle/iStockphoto. (bcr) ©Fotokostic/Shutterstock. (bkg) ©Joel Sartore/National Geographic Stock. (bl) ©Marvin Dembinsky Photo Associates/Alamy. (br) ©Layer, Werner/Animals Animals/Earth Scenes. **181** (bc) ©Peter Anderson/Dorling Kindersley/Getty Images. (cl) ©Robert Maier/Animals Animals. (cr) ©Denis and Yulia Pogostins/Shutterstock. (tc) ©PhotoDisc/Getty Images. **182** (bkg) ©Ariusz Nawrocki/iStockphoto. **184** (bcl) ©Harry Rogers/Photo Researchers, Inc. (bcr) ©John Mitchell/Photo Researchers, Inc. (bkg) ©Ethan Meleg/All Canada Photos/Corbis. (bl) ©Gregory K. Scott/Photo Researchers, Inc. (br) ©jack thomas/Alamy. (tc) ©David M. Dennis/Animals Animals. **185** (bc) ©Robert Lubeck/Animals Animals. (cl) ©Gary Neil Corbett/Superstock, Inc. (cr) ©E. R. Degginger/Photo Researchers. **186** (bkg) ©Don Johnston/Alamy. (bl) ©Skip Moody-Rainbow/Science Faction/Getty Images. (br) ©Thomas Kitchin & Victoria Hurst/First Light/Getty Images. (cl) ©Specker, Donald/Animals Animals - Earth Scenes. (cr) ©Skip Moody-Rainbow/Science Faction/Getty Images. **187** (cl) ©Thomas Kitchin & Victoria Hurst/First Light/Getty Images. (cr) ©Thomas Kitchin & Victoria Hurst/First Light/Getty Images. (tl) ©Don Farrall/Getty Images. **188** (bkg) ©Emil von Maltitz/Gallo Images/Getty Images. (bl) ©Sanchez, Juan M. & De Lope, Jose L./Animals Animals - Earth Scenes. (cl) ©Joœl Hœras/Bios/photolibrary.com. (cr) ©Sanchez, Juan M. & De Lope, Jose L./Animals Animals - Earth Scenes. **189** (c) ©Medford Taylor/National Geographic Stock. **190** (bc) ©Bert Pijs/FN/Minden Pictures/National Geographic Stock. (bl) ©Alex Wild/Visuals Unlimited/Corbis. (br) ©Dr Jeremy Burgess/Science Photo Library/Photo Researchers. (cl) ©Dr Jeremy Burgess/Science Photo Library/Photo. Researchers (tbl) ©Bert Pijs/FN/Minden Pictures/National Geographic Stock. (tl) ©Perennou Nuridsany/Photo Researchers, Inc. **191** (cl) ©Herbert Reimann/age footstock. (tbl) ©Imagebroker/Alamy. (tl) ©Rene Krekels/Foto Nature/Minden Pictures/National Geographic Stock. **192** (cl) ©Elizabeth Howard/University of Minnesota Monarch Lab/Karen S. Oberhauser. (tl) ©David Stuckel/Alamy. **193** (bkg) ©Paul Sutherland/National Geographic Stock (bl) ©Raul Gonzalez Perez/Photo Researchers, Inc.

End Matter
194 (bkg) ©Radius Images/Corbis. **196** (b) ©Lana Sundman/Alamy. **197** (b) ©Lana Sundman/Alamy. **198** (bl) ©Tom Wagner/Alamy. **199** (tr) ©Robert Pickett/Papilio/Alamy.

Photo Studio images © National Geographic Learning, Cengage Learning.

PROGRAM CONSULTANTS

Randy Bell, Ph.D.
Associate Professor of Science Education,
University of Virginia, Charlottesville, Virginia
SCIENCE

Kathy Cabe Trundle, Ph.D.
Associate Professor of Early Childhood
Science Education,
The School of Teaching and Learning,
The Ohio State University, Columbus, Ohio
SCIENCE

Judith Sweeney Lederman, Ph.D.
Director of Teacher Education,
Associate Professor of Science Education,
Department of Mathematics and
Science Education,
Illinois Institute of Technology, Chicago, Illinois
SCIENCE

David W. Moore, Ph.D.
Professor of Education,
Mary Lou Fulton Teachers College,
Arizona State University, Tempe, Arizona
LITERACY

PROGRAM CONTRIBUTOR

Cathey Whitener, M.S. in Ed.
Science Specialist,
Marcella Intermediate School,
Aldine ISD, Houston, Texas
SCIENCE

Acknowledgments
Grateful acknowledgment is given to the authors, artists, photographers, museums, publishers, and agents for permission to reprint copyrighted material. Every effort has been made to secure the appropriate permission. If any omissions have been made or if corrections are required, please contact the Publisher.

STAAR is a trademark and/or federally registered trademark owned by the Texas Education Agency, and is used pursuant to license.

Photographic Credits
Front cover ©Tim Fitzharris/Minden Pictures/National Geographic Stock, (bkg) © Seide Preis/Getty Images.
Back cover © Tim Fitzharris/Minden Pictures/National Geographic Stock.

Illustrator Credit
Precision Graphics.

Maps Credit
Mapping Specialists.

Acknowledgments and credits continued on page 204.

For permission to use material from this text or product, submit all requests online at www.cengage.com/permissions

Further permissions questions can be emailed to permissionrequest@cengage.com

Visit National Geographic Learning online at www.NGSP.com

Visit our corporate website at www.cengage.com

Printed in the USA.
RR Donnelley, Jefferson City, MO

ISBN: 978-07362-93921

12 13 14 15 16 17 18 19 20 21

10 9 8 7 6 5 4 3 2 1